PARENT POWER: A GUIDE TO RESPONSIBLE CHILDREARING

Parent Power
A
Guide to
Responsible Childrearing

By
LOGAN WRIGHT
University of Oklahoma

LOGAN WRIGHT FOUNDATION
2627 Silvertree Drive
Oklahoma City, OK 73120

Printed in the United States of America

1 9 8 7 6 5 4 3 2 1

Library of Congress Cataloging in Publication Data

Wright, Logan, 1933-
    Parent power.

    Bibliography: p.
    Includes index.
    1. Children--Management. I. Title.
HQ769.W8794   649'.1   77-28100
ISBN 0-88437-014-3

DEDICATION

This book is dedicated to a person who has overcome great hardship. Growing up amidst the trials of farm life at the turn of the century, she lost her only brothers to terrible and unnecessary deaths: tetanus, and a trampling by a horse. When her husband died, all he left her was a fatherless child. Despite the Great Depression, she found a meager-paying job, and with the advent of World War II her earnings rose to almost $100.00 a month. Somehow, she not only reared her child, but instilled in him an unwavering sense of security and hope. I dedicate this book to that woman and her unique love, which sped the process of growth during my younger years, and which now slows the inevitable consequences of that process as I begin to age: To My Mother.

ABOUT THE AUTHOR

Logan Wright has devoted his entire career to understanding and helping both children and parents in trouble. His research and teaching activities with children and parents have been extensive. A partial list of his activities shows that he has taught, lectured, and written on such subjects as mental retardation, battered children, death and dying, respiration, disturbed children, personality development and integration, psychomotor learning in children, measurement of personality growth, intelligence, overachievement and underachievement, sleep, athletic and physical education in human development, psychotherapy with parents and children, and specific behavioral disorders: habitual vomiting, self-induced seizures, lead poisoning, encopresis, drug habituation, tracheostomy, bruxism.

The author received his Ph.D. from George Peabody College and has previously taught at Bethel College and Purdue University. He also has been named a Career Development Research Fellow by the National Institute of Health. Currently he is Head of the Division of Pediatric Psychology at the University of Oklahoma Medical School.

But most importantly, the author has successfully survived the onslaught of raising three children himself.

Contents

PREFACE

Childrearing is big business. Over fifty million Americans are engaged in the process of rearing or otherwise refining over seventy-five million youngsters under age fifteen. Clearly this is our nation's largest enterprise; it is also the most important.

Whether this nation flourishes or founders depends upon the character of its citizens. And nothing is more important in determining the character of a generation than the quality of childrearing it receives. Dr. Ernest Fremont Tittle writes that "every new generation is a fresh invasion of savages." It is the adults of the present generation, the parents, who are largely responsible for civilizing tomorrow's adults.

In spite of the obvious importance of childrearing, resources in this area are about as scarce as parts for a Packard. Only a few colleges offer courses in childrearing, and these are usually taught only to those majoring in home economics. This condemns the rest of us not only to the preparation of nutritionless meals, but to the most unruly of children.

I have spent much of my time over the past decade consulting with parents who were having difficulty with their children. Through that experience I have come to understand the kinds of skills parents most often lack. Most parents are well equipped to love their children, but love isn't enough. There are certain principles of behavior that cannot be ignored, and these translate into principles of childrearing. Many of the principles are common sense, and in many cases the parent is not so much unaware of the principle as he or she is unaware of how it is applied. In my work with parents, I concentrate on helping parents master these principles and their application to common everyday problems. This book is an attempt to offer the same kind of information to you.

But unlike nearly every other childrearing book, this book is NOT for everybody. It is only for parents. Not only that, it is only for parents who take childrearing seriously, who consider it a challenge they want to meet, head-on. And it is a book that places the responsibility for childrearing where it belongs—with the parents.

Sloan Wilson, author of *The Man in the Gray Flannel Suit,* has said: "I was extremely thankful for the fact that my children turned out to be rebels, not against society, but against me, and all the permissive fathers like me. Somebody, they said, had to set the rules, and if I couldn't, they would. . . . If kids realized how little their parents know and how little self-confidence any intelligent mother or father has, they would be too scared to grow up at all."

In my years as a child therapist, I've become more and more concerned with the guilt parents feel about assuming authority and responsibility for their children. Something in American society has made us feel that we're wrong to make rules or set limits and enforce them. I believe that children not only thrive with firm parenting, but actually appreciate it. In homes where the children have all the power, both parent and child suffer. The child is robbed of the security and confidence that come from having strong adults to care for him, but is left instead with a peer, and not an ordinary peer, but one he can manipulate. Everybody loses. But if parents can take professional knowledge and combine it with the love they naturally bring to their children, that should be an unbeatable combination for effective childrearing. So, if you are reading this book out of love for your children, and I imagine you are, then together we should make a good combination.

To be fair, however, I must also admit my weaknesses. For one, I'm prejudiced. I was born in the Southwest and I share all the middle class prejudices about what kids should have, like allowances and privacy and three meals a day. If you come from the Upper East Side of New York, you may not catch all my jokes. And if you come from the ghetto, you may laugh at some of my examples. "Hey," you may say, "that's not my world." Sorry about that, but I can only give you illustrations from the world I've experienced. If I tried to talk in Rolls-Royce terms or use ghetto imagery, I would come off sounding phony. What I have to say may sound a little odd, like an unfamiliar accent, but I think that under our accents, we have a lot in common.

As a middle-aged American, I am, of course, sexist. I try not to be, but I can't help it. I grew up thinking that boys were boys and girls were girls and the twain should never meet—except under carefully prescribed circumstances. I thought sex referred to the making of babies, with instruments ill-suited to the task. I'm exaggerating, of course, and I have tried to change with the times. But I'm sure that some feminists will find fault with my examples. To demonstrate my good faith, I first wrote this entire manuscript without ever using the specified pronoun "he." It was she/he this and he/she that and his/her this and her/his that and him/her this and so on. The trouble is, all that slashing gets in the way of understanding what the sentence is trying to say. And to be truly non-sexist, you'd have to say she/he fifty percent of the time and he/she fifty percent of the time; you'd have to make sure the he/she's didn't outnumber the she/he's. So I threw up my hands and went traditional, sexist or not. If you're offended, I'm sorry.

Most of the time I talk to the reader as though he or she were one of a pair. I spend a lot of my time working with parents, trying to increase their skills in dealing with their children. I *know*, however, that there are a lot of families that consist of only one parent, or only grandparents, or one parent and one in-law and so on. Most kids still grow up in homes where there is one father and one mother, but more and more are growing up in homes where the father is gone most of the time (as when the parents are separated or divorced), where there was never a father, where both parents have turned the child over to grandparents, or where there is a kind of friendly arrangement in which 4 or 5 or 6 or 50 people are involved, in one way or another, in the care of a child. I'm not condemning any of these modes of childrearing, though I confess I'm partial to the traditional two-parent arrangement. The point is that you can't write a book specifically for all these kinds of arrangements at once, so what I focused on were those in the traditional (and still most common) setup.

Now, in spite of the prejudices I've confessed, and despite the limitations of this book, I think it can help you. Because even if my examples seem a little far-fetched to you or you get annoyed by my sexist language or you wish I'd stop assuming there are two of you when you're all by yourself—in spite of all this, the principles which I describe really work. They are based on theories that psychiatrists and psychologists have been using for years. I have tried to express the principles in plain English without a lot of fancy words or tables and graphs to muddle your head. (After all, you've got a kid to muddle your head for you.) But I will be forced on occasions to use jargon (the "mumbo jumbo" language of a given specialty). The law field has its "amicus curiae" and "corpus delicti"; the space program has given us such gems as "apogee" and "telemetry." Psychology, of course, is not to be left out. We have responded with words like "anthropomorphizing" and "acrophobia." My goal is to present you with information that is usually reserved for professional therapists and consultants, so a certain amount of psychologese is required.

Since I know that some of you will wonder, let me reassure you that I *am* a parent, the father of two sons and a daughter whose ages range from seventeen to twenty-one. These children have provided my most crucial tests and deeply personal experiences with a principles-oriented approach to childrearing. It is with the greatest of personal joy that I observe in their emerging character and behavior the most conclusive validation of the effectiveness of the principles I offer you in this book.

A very special acknowledgement is gratefully given to Mr. Paul Chance without whose editing and organizational refinement this book would not have been possible. I would like to thank Lois Fagin for her extremely valuable suggestions concerning this book. I would also like to acknowledge with grateful appreciation the contribution of a devoted secretary, Deanna Warshell. She has typed and retyped the most scribbled of manuscripts, corrected innumerable "mis-pelled" (sic) words, and persevered at what must have been the world's most boring job. To my wife, Pat, and our children, Brooks, Jaye, and Blaine, I offer a special thanks for walking quietly through the house, foregoing group activities and otherwise being super good sports because, "Dad's writing a book."

My goal is to present you with a short, understandable handbook filled with practical principles about kids. That's what I've tried to do. If it helps, let me know; if it doesn't, let me know that, too. Either way, I look forward to hearing from you.

Logan Wright

1

Who's In Charge Here

The order of the day for any parent who wants to retain some semblance of sanity is to get and maintain control. But the most important reason for seizing control is that *you must be able to control a child before you can really support and love him*. If they are to feel secure, children need parents who are effective, who cannot be manipulated. Children look down on adults they can manipulate and control. The love, encouragement, or praise coming from such parents therefore has little impact on a child.

Another reason we must control our children has to do with our reaction when they manipulate us. We tend to feel both ineffective and angry, making it difficult to be supportive or to even *want* to be. On the other hand, if we feel more content and adequate, we are free to use our energies in support of our children rather than to protect ourselves from their manipulations.

We hear a lot about democratic styles of childrearing. One person, one vote. That may be okay when the adult to child split is two to one or better, but after that, look out, you might wind up with a scenario such as this:

"Mom and Dad, we've taken a vote and decided that this family should move."

"Move? But we haven't even been asked for our votes."

"Mary, Billy, and I all vote for Venezuela. That makes it three to two. We go to Venezuela."

"Venezuela?"

"By Friday."

"Friday? Why so soon?"

"Why not? Besides, I have this test in history next Monday."

Admittedly an extreme example, but not beyond the realm of possibility if parents were to carry the democratic view of childrearing to its logical end.

Then there are people who worry obsessively about the adverse effects of parental control. Never say "no" to a child, they argue. You'll stunt his curiosity, you'll suppress his natural tendency to explore. The sight of your little darling sprawled on the kitchen floor amid the contents of the day's garbage may raise your blood pressure, but you're supposed to remember that this is a creative endeavor, an exploration of the world. That's not your four-year-old messing up a freshly waxed floor, it's Leonardo da Vinci, preparing for a magnificent future. Is your precious boy writing four-letter words on the wall? Let him; he's only practicing free expression.

Bunk. Sure, children should be allowed freedom. Certainly they ought to participate in some decisions that affect the family. And, yes, children are people and have rights. But a naively democratic approach neglects the fact that parents are people too, and they also have rights. More importantly, parents have responsibilities. Someone has to be in charge.

Like it or not, until the little cherubs reach the age of majority, you are responsible for their care and safety. And you are responsible for their behavior. You will have to answer for the windows he breaks hitting fly balls, the dresses she ruins playing doctor. And when they're older and their entertainment becomes more expensive, you will share the blame if their games and pranks end up as traffic accidents or worse:

"But, Your Honor. I *asked* Mary not to play with the car. I warned her that she might cause an accident. She just wouldn't listen to me. What could I do?" The judge may decide you can either pay up or do several years in prison.

Parents must take charge in order to meet their responsibilities to the child and to society. But the main reason that parents need to be in control is for the psychological benefit of the child. The first principle of childrearing is that:

Children Need Adult Leadership

Every child needs someone who is more capable, more stable, and stronger than himself. He needs someone who has had the experiences that bring self-confidence and the maturity to think things through and make rational decisions.

When children dominate their parents, they make orphans of themselves and babies of their parents. Nobody wants to be an orphan, figuratively or literally. And although children may resist having power wrestled from them, they will welcome having someone else to rely upon. It takes a long time to develop the intellectual and social skills that mark an adult, and it is frightening to be on your own before you are ready for it. Probably the saddest and most frequent monologue comes from kids who have gone "wrong." The details may vary, but it usually runs like this:

"The trouble with my parents was, they never gave me any real direction. They were too soft. I could get anything I wanted if I bluffed them long enough, and I never really had to do anything. Other kids thought it was great, but I envied kids with tougher parents. *They* knew who was boss and what was what."

Children who lack parental leadership are always at their parents, pushing, tugging, arguing—forever testing, searching for the boundaries that will allow them to relax with the clear and comfortable knowledge of exactly what they can and cannot get away with. The harder these limits are to establish, the more unruly and unhappy the children will be. Not just because a lack of leadership allows chaos to reign (which it does) but because kids need limits that will tell

2

them what they are competent to do for themselves and what adults must still do for them. Controlling adults isn't good for children, but like heroin, it can be addictive. They can't even partake in moderation, much less leave it alone. They get hooked on manipulating parents even though no one enjoys it and certainly no one benefits. Without leadership, without rules, without limits, no family can function, any more than a country, state or local chapter of the PTA can function without leadership and direction.

The family may be a cocoon that insulates the child from the demands of reality, but eventually those realities must be faced. A child who has never had to live with rules, who has never had to meet responsibilities, to give as well as receive, is in no condition to go off on his own.

The home must provide a training ground for adult life, a laboratory where the child experiments and finds out at minimal cost what works and what doesn't. Parents should make the home as much like the outside world as possible. In the real world there are payoffs for good work and a price to pay for bad work.

You finished that report on time, or even ahead of time? You'll probably get a word of praise, a pat on the back, and maybe a bonus or a raise from your boss.

You were studying the racing form and the report is late? No raise, no pat on the back. Probably no job, either.

Little Suzy cleaned her room, and without even being reminded? Lots of praise, more time to play, and maybe a bonus in her allowance.

Little Suzy's room looks like the aftermath of a twister and her homework is collecting cobwebs? No praise for that, and no watching *Star Trek*, either. In short, life is full of responsibilities. As Robert Frost writes:

I have promises to keep
And miles to go before I sleep
And miles to go before I sleep

Frost's poem is not about a person used to having things his own way, used to being waited on hand and foot. It is about someone with responsibilities, promises to keep. "We'd like to lead," you say, "but will our kids let us?" The answer is no if you begin on such an insecure basis. You must make a commitment to succeed.

"Don't saddle a horse you can't ride," an old-timer used to tell me. Some problems are going to be stubborn. If you are not determined to stay with it, don't bother to begin. If you follow the principles in this book two days out of four, you won't get good results; you'll get bedlam. So make up your mind now who is going to rear your children—you or they.

All right, so you've decided it should be you. Where do you begin? Begin with yourself. If you are a single parent, in some ways your job may be easier. If there is a grandparent or other relative who will be involved actively with the children, make sure that they are "with you," for if they aren't with you, they are definitely against you.

Two intelligent, well-motivated adults who go about the childrearing business in different ways are fighting themselves. "Some single mind," wrote Abraham Lincoln during the Civil War, "must be master, else there will be no agreement on anything." Lincoln's advice was good for getting a nation through a violent war and, with a little luck, it will also help you get through the years of childrearing with a minimum of bloodshed. Read this book carefully, discuss the rules and principles between yourselves, and try to reach a mutual understanding of exactly what each principle means and how it applies to specific problems in your *home*.

You will find differences of opinion. One parent will want to use corporal punishment, another will not. One will like the idea of using tokens (chapter four), another will think this too materialistic. It may be tempting to overlook these differences, especially if the two of you see eye to eye on most topics. But it's important that you resolve your differences, that you work out compromises. If you don't, sooner or later the kids will find those differences and home in on them.

Some parents hate to have these discussions because they haven't really thought through their childrearing practices, and discussions will reveal the flaws and inconsistencies in their views. I remember a country lady with a hint of Ma Kettle in her voice and a simple, direct way of expressing herself:

"I've tried to talk to Albert (her husband) about the children. He tells 'em one thing one day, and sump'n else the next. Some days he just don't do nothin', and lets 'em run all over him. Tryin' to get him to agree to sump'n and stick by it is like tryin' to nail jello to a tree."

I hated to tell her, but there's no substitute for such discussions. If parents are going to lead, there must be some agreement about where they're headed.

This book, if it doesn't do anything else, will help by giving you something concrete to fight about. Instead of arguing about your own parental practices, you can begin by kicking around one of my principles. That will eventually lead to a discussion of your own views on its interpretation and application, and *that's* going to prove to be really beneficial.

You might start by kicking around the principle that parents should take charge. How much control should parents have? How much freedom should children have? Should children have any vote in what the family does? These are questions no professional can answer for you. You and other adults who are responsible for the rearing of your children must decide these matters for yourselves.

The best way to do this is to sit down and talk. Or stand up and talk. Or go for a walk and talk. BUT TALK.

Once you've had your first talk and you've come to some agreement, you're ready to go on. Let's presume you will have decided that the first principle, that children need adult leadership, is essentially correct. *You,* not the kids, are to be in charge of childrearing. But how does one take charge of something so global and diffuse? Where do you begin?

A good place to start is by understanding that your child is not a Buick.

Focus On Behavior

You get up on a cold wintry morning and go out to start your old Buick. You try to crank it up, but instead of behaving properly, the car moans in disobedience, "Nnnnnnnnnnoooooooooo Ch-chug, chug, chug, oooooooh." You can't blame it for not wanting to start right up when it's five degrees below zero, but you have to get to work. You try again. "Ohhhhhnnnnnyyyoo, ch, ch, ch, ch, cough, cough." And so on. It won't start, so you begin thinking, "What's wrong with this thing, why won't it go? What does it need?" You start looking for some deficiency, for something that the car needs in order to run. Does it need a Die Hard battery? Is the wiring faulty? You do this because this sort of diagnostic, what-does-it-need approach works. Using that approach, you eventually find out that the car is out of gas or the battery is dry or the distributor cap has moisture under it. You correct the flaw, and the car starts. If you can't find out what the car needs, you call in an expert who goes through a more sophisticated search.

Parents typically assume the same approach will work in childrearing. Find out what the child needs, meet that need, and the problem will go away. Rick is swinging from the chandeliers? He's telling you he needs something, the logic goes, and you have to figure out what it is. Maybe it's attention. Or maybe it's affection. Or maybe a new toy. The trouble is that a child is not a Buick. (You can tell because an automobile has a much higher trade-in value.)

We got started on treating children like cars by, of all people, the disciples of Sigmund Freud. "If ze child ist zvinging from ze chandeliers," they would say, "zen you must find out vat ist goink on in his unconscious head to make him vant to do zis ridiculous zing."

Then they would suggest a list of possibilities: he is in love with his mother, he hates his father, the chandeliers symbolize genitals and swinging on them is a way of masturbating metaphorically. Maybe so. But how does this help you keep your child from swinging on the chandeliers?

And that's my point: trying to figure out *why* a child does something, what needs drive him to do a thing, is often a waste of time.

For one thing, there are usually many reasons for a child's behavior, not just one. For another thing, even if you figure out what causes a particular behavior, that doesn't insure that you will have a solution.

If you determine that your car isn't running because it's out of gas, the cause suggests a solution. But if your analyst tells you that your child's chandelier swinging is symbolic masturbation, what do you do? The supposed "cause" doesn't suggest a solution.

This book has a strongly pragmatic orientation. If you want to read about the machinations that go on in the deep dark recesses of your child's mind, you should be reading another book (perhaps *The Exorcist*). This book is not about to tell you what the chandelier swinging symbolizes or what it indicates a child needs; this book is concerned with another, simpler question: how do you get the kid to stop swinging on the chandeliers? If that issue is the one that concerns you the most, then principle number two will be of interest to you:

It's What The Child <u>Does</u> That Counts

The nice thing about this principle is that it allows you to make use of all of the other principles in this book. Put another way, if you ignore this principle, if you persist in trying to get inside your child's head, you may as well not read any further. You cannot make use of the principles that follow unless you are willing to focus on behavior. Some deep thinking and very with-it people will find this approach naive. If you don't look for the cause, they reason, you'll never get anywhere. But ignoring the cause and focusing on the behavior itself does work. For example, one of the most severe childhood problems is autism. Autistic children hardly act human: they have little or no speech, hate to be held, don't respond to questions or commands, avoid eye contact, don't seem to recognize their parents or others they see everyday. Sometimes they are destructive: they bite people, tear curtains from windows, smear their feces on the walls. Sometimes they bite themselves, and hit their heads on a wall or the side of a desk.

Autism is an extreme problem for a parent, or professional, to deal with; probably the most difficult a parent can face.

People used to think they knew what caused autism. A psychologist named Bruno Bettelheim treated a number of autistic children and he began to see—or so he thought—a pattern in the parents of these children. The parents seemed to be cool, intellectual people who had difficulty giving love freely. He theorized that these parents felt ambivalent about their children, both loving and rejecting them at the same time. They communicated this ambivalence, said Bettelheim, in the way they held the child. The parents might vigorously deny it, but the infant—highly sensitive to such nonverbal communication—would detect it.

The child, feeling he was in a hostile, rejecting world, would retreat from it. He would not communicate with other people, would not even recognize their existence. He would create a fortress against the rest of the world and live within it among fantasies.

Since the cause of autism, according to Bettelheim, was a lack of love, the cure must be more love. Bettelheim treated autistic children by hugging them, talking to them, never scolding or rejecting them. The child is banging his head against the wall? Quick, run over and give him a hug.

Bettelheim's theory sounds very believable, and he even felt that his therapy produced cures. Then came Ivar Lovaas, a psychologist at UCLA. He tried Bettelheim's theory. One day,quite by accident,he found that a child who banged her head on a cabinet would stop doing so if he gave her a slap on the bottom.

Lavaas began to collect data. When a child would bang his head, someone would run to him and hug him. Head banging increased. Then they tried punishing head banging. Its frequency dropped off.

None of this made any sense if Bettelheim's theory were correct. From head banging and other self-destructive behavior, Lovaas and his colleagues went on to developing language skills, increasing eye contact, and improving interactions with others.

The point is that from the standpoint of the parent who has to deal with a child right here, right now, theorizing about causes and cures has little practical value. It makes little difference *why* Linda is playing on the roof. The problems are, in order of importance: how to get her down without breaking her neck, and how to discourage her from getting up there again.

In spite of the fact that figuring out causes will seldom help in solving problems, some parents can produce more interpretations than a Monday-morning quarterback. But their gems of insight often get in the way more than a blitzing linebacker.

Martin: (age four) I want some ice cream.

Mother: Fine, I'll get it for you.

Martin: (after receiving two scoops of chocolate ripple) I don't want that. I don't like that old brown stuff.

Mother: That's the only kind of ice cream we have.

Martin: I'm not gonna eat it. (pushes bowl away)

Mother: I should have known this would happen. You're always this way when you don't have a nap.

Even though Martin's mother may have made an accurate interpretation of why little Martin was irritable, interpreting the behavior accomplished nothing. It diverted attention from the practical matter of what Martin did, and redirected it toward the origin of his behavior. The situation might have been better handled this way:

Martin: I want some ice cream.

Mother: Fine, I'll get it for you.

Martin: I don't want that ice cream. I don't like that old brown stuff.

Mother: That's the only kind of ice cream we have.

Martin: Then I'm not going to eat it.

Mother: I'm really sorry about that. But let me remind you that if you ask for food and don't eat it, you don't get dessert at the next meal.

This time the parent is dealing with reality—Martin's behavior—not with conjectures about the effects of naps. This is not to say that if Mom or Dad notices a persistent tendency for Martin to be irritable when he skips his nap, that they should ignore it. They may decide that they should never allow Martin to miss a nap. Fine. But when Martin is behaving badly, it makes little difference if it is because of a missed nap or a full moon. The behavior is the problem, not the nap or the need for attention or an oedipal complex or what it is about chocolate ripple that turns Martin off.

Some parents (in fact, some psychotherapists) argue that behavior is only a symptom. If you focus on the behavior, they argue, you miss the more important underlying conflict. And, they continue, even if you change the behavior, the underlying cause will still be there, and will eventually cause other problems. This is known as symptom substitution. The idea is that problem behavior is like a worn out tire. You patch that leak and another one appears.

Like Bettelheim's theory of autism, this view sounds reasonable. Fortunately for parents, the facts do not fit the theory. Studies have been conducted to determine how often symptom substitution occurs. These studies show that it occurs less than two percent of the time. That is, for every 100 instances in which behavior was dealt with and changed, new symptoms took their place only twice.

There are a couple of other good reasons for focusing on symptoms (behavior) instead of searching for their causes. First, the symptoms may actually be more important than the unconscious psychodynamics that are supposed to be responsible for the symptoms. For instance, if a child of four takes up playing with matches it could be downright dangerous to search for underlying causes. While you're trying to figure out what flames symbolize in the child's unconscious, he may incinerate half a block.

Another reason for focusing on behavior is that the behavior may outlast its causes, hence the cause may be irrelevant. For example, a child may be upset on a given day and talk rudely to a parent or become destructive. If the parents spend all of their energy speculating about the child's problems without responding to the behavior, the child may get in the habit of being rude or destructive. He may continue to act this way even when not upset. In such cases, an attack upon the symptom rather than its origin would obviously be more beneficial.

Another form of the theory that you have to change underlying causes to get changes in behavior is the idea of reasoning with the child. Somehow, many people have gotten the idea that a good parent is one who reasons with the child. Change the child's attitudes and the behavior will change all by itself. The only trouble is that it works the other way around! Change a person's behavior and changes in attitude follow.

Words, in fact, may be the most over-estimated commodity in today's market. Parents who focus on behavior allow their child to learn by experience. They realize that comments of admonition or persuasion are best left unsaid unless they provide *new* information. Statements like, "If you don't make good grades you won't get into the college of your choice," should be made only once; after that, it's not new information. Can you imagine what it would be like in most homes if this rule were strictly followed? Many parents would have withdrawal symptoms. We'd have to start a new organization called "Naggers Anonymous." A parent could call up a friend every time he felt like blurting out favorite redundancies such as, "If you smoke it will stunt your growth," or "If you don't eat, you'll grow up to be a midget," or "If you wet the bed once more, a rainbow will follow you around the rest of your life," or the old standby, "Be careful, you never know what a little innocent petting will lead to." Then the friend could come over, and the two of them would drink together until the urge to nag went away. All of this could go a long way toward enabling parents to reclaim their most important role: a provider of *experiences* (not talk) for their children.

You have a girl who would rather play softball than study? The "reasoning" parent would sit down and have a heart-to-heart talk with her. He would explain that studying might not always be fun, but it is important. One must learn to accept responsibilities, to do what's necessary. And people who don't study don't get ahead in life. They have trouble getting into college and trade schools or getting accepted for jobs. The parent may speak eloquently, his arguments may be terrific, and they may even spur the child to new efforts. Temporarily. But to get permanent changes, you have to focus *on the behavior*. Long lectures intended to change a child's thoughts are not likely to change his behavior.

Another example comes from race relations. People used to think that you had to change racial attitudes, then there would be fair treatment in housing, hiring, and other areas. But, it just doesn't work that way. Now we recognize that when laws guarantee fair treatment in housing and employment and other areas, *then* attitudes begin to change.

In sum, it's what people *do* that counts. So focus on behavior, not attitudes, psychological needs, unconscious forces, psychodynamics and other "causes." Focus on what the child *does*.

Okay, so now you're focusing your attention on what the child does. And you're finding that he often does things which seem adaptive, but not as often as you'd like. What next?

The next step is obvious.

Join the Scouts.

3

Reward Virtue

The Boy Scouts and Girl Scouts of America are supposed to be good-deed-doers. They are a force of mini-Supermen and mini-Superwomen, forever vigilant, forever seeking to reward virtue and punish vice. (This is probably not, strictly speaking, what the Scout oath says, but it's close enough to suit my purposes.) Anyway, I want you to be something of a Scout. But relax, I would never be so idealistic as to ask a parent to be "courteous, trustworthy, brave, and true." I'm not even asking you to be forever vigilant. I'll be happy if you'll keep in mind the part about rewarding virtue. (Don't worry about punishing vice. That comes later.)

What I'm suggesting is that while you're busy concentrating on behavior, you pay particular attention to *good* behavior. Oddly enough, this is probably the place where most parents get into trouble. They're always on the alert for misbehavior, and they develop a kind of special sense for detecting trouble:

"Johnny, you're being awfully quiet in there. What are you up to?"

"Your room looks really great. Hmmmm. Is this report card day?"

"Flowers?? For me?. . . . . What have you done now?"

Some parents are busier than a cow's tail in the summer looking for bad behavior—so busy, in fact, that they ignore good behavior. To see more good behavior, you have to follow principle number three:

Behavior That is Rewarded Tends to be Repeated

In other words, when Junior behaves well, do something Junior likes. This principle, you will say, is obviously too simple to produce results. Surely it's more complicated than that. Why else would parents have such difficulty getting their children to make their beds, be ready for school on time, or pick up their toys?

Nevertheless, study after study has shown that the proper use of this principle can radically improve the behavior of even the most difficult children. It may even help *your* kids.

First, you need to understand what a reward is and how it should be used. Psychologists call rewards "positive reinforcers" because they strengthen or reinforce the behavior they follow. A reward, then, is anything that increases the likelihood that a behavior will reoccur.

Your paycheck makes it likely that you will return to work next week. If the paychecks stopped coming, the chances that you would go to the factory or office would drop off sharply. Money is one well known, reliable reinforcer or reward. There are thousands of others. All of them can be classified as either primary or secondary reinforcers.

Primary reinforcers are unlearned. Food, for example, is a primary reinforcer. So are water, air, sleep, and sex. They can be very effective rewards.

For example, in chapter two we talked about autism, and I mentioned that autistic children do not make eye contact with other people. To them, a person is just another object occupying space.

In accordance with principle two (focus on behavior) psychologists have tried to increase eye contact. They do this by rewarding eye contact with *primary reinforcers*. Each time the child turns in the direction of the therapist, the therapist gives him a piece of cookie or an M&M. Pretty soon, the child is looking right into the therapist's eyes. Already he is less autistic.

But primary reinforcers have rather severe limitations, especially for older children who live at home rather than in hospitals. For one thing, food isn't reinforcing unless a child is hungry. I know that you might think that your child could eat M&M's all day, but try it sometime and you'll find he gets tired of them pretty quickly.

Another problem with primary reinforcers is that they are often inconvenient. If you are driving down the road and you want to reinforce Johnny's good manners, it may not be convenient to pull out a bag of M&M's and give him a couple.

Because of these and other limitations, primary reinforcers are ordinarily useful only with very young children, or children with severe behavior problems—the autistic, the mentally retarded, etc. And, even in these special cases, therapists try to shift as quickly as possible to *secondary reinforcers*.

A secondary reinforcer is one that is learned. It does not reduce any specific biological need the way food and water do. Secondary reinforcers include most of the good things in life: attention, praise, success, hugs, and kisses.

Most of us, as adults, get all the primary reinforcers we want. Our behavior is more often shaped by the desire for secondary reinforcers. We want fame, riches, and romance. Fortunately, your child will settle for a lot less: praise, a toy, or a little affection.

It doesn't take an expert to notice that most people like attention or that people like to be praised for their efforts. Used correctly, these and other secondary reinforcers can be extremely powerful tools for changing a child's behavior from infancy until the day he leaves the nest. When I tell parents the principles of reward and about primary and secondary reinforcers, I often hear something like this:

"Big deal. I've known that since I was ten. That's just common sense."

But before you join them and skip to the next chapter, bear with me a little bit longer. The principle may sound simple, but its application requires some sophistication.

Praise or other rewards from one individual may be scoffed at, while the same reaction from others is genuinely appreciated. The important factor seems to be whether or not the parent is *giving* to the child or *extracting* from him. All this reminds me of the case of young Jennifer who refused to take her medication. She was quickly conditioned by a hospital technician to accept twelve bitter-tasting pills per day. After the technician had succeeded in securing the child's cooperation, an attempt was made to have the mother perform this task. But as soon as the mother began to administer the pills and the reinforcer (which consisted of a hug and the statement, "That's good"), the child ceased to cooperate. She would throw the pills on the floor and if an attempt was made to force a pill down, she would spit it out. Mother responded by trying to coax Jennifer into taking the medication; next she resorted to shaming her, and eventually to threatening the child. Obviously this mother was greatly lacking in social reinforcement skills, so an attempt was made to train her. The first lesson was in letting the reinforcer speak for itself, rather than coaxing, shaming or threatening. Mother was shown how coaxing could reinforce *not* taking the pills, since this allowed Jennifer to manipulate and control.

The second lesson involved the flavor of communication between mother and daughter. Mother seemed to be extracting from Jennifer rather than giving to her, as though the mother needed affection and approval from the child. Jennifer, of course, sensed this and came to feel that closeness meant daughter gave to mother rather than the other way around. This made contact with mother a giving rather than a receiving of reinforcement. After the mother was coached on interactional skills, the medication was given successfully.

Remember, I said that you should focus on behavior—that means *your* behavior as well as the child's. Reinforcing or rewarding a child's behavior means changing *your* behavior. So you see, the principle that good acts should be rewarded has to do as much with your behavior as it does with that of your child. An example may help:

A nursery school teacher had a lot of trouble with Billy. The other children played together nicely, but this little boy was always disrupting the other children's games. If a child was building a sand castle, Billy would run over and knock it down. If two children were playing with toy trucks, Billy would run away with their toys.

The nursery school teacher, who knew a thing or two about psychological theory, reasoned: "This child is starved for attention. Perhaps his parents don't give him enough attention at home, so when he comes here he tries to get attention from his teacher and the other children by being disruptive."

Since the cause was a lack of attention, obviously the cure was to provide plenty of attention. Every time Billy would steal another child's toy or hit another child, she would run to him. "Billy, let's play," she would say. The trouble was, Billy continued to be disruptive. In fact, he seemed to be getting worse.

Then another teacher recommended a different tactic. "Forget about trying to figure out *why* Billy misbehaves," he suggested. "Concentrate on what he *does* and on what you do. When he misbehaves, try going away, give attention to someone who is playing properly. Give Billy attention *only* when he is playing well by himself or with others."

This advice made no sense in terms of the "needs attention" theory, but the teacher decided she'd try it. In a week or two, Billy was a new little man. No more hitting, much less disruptive play.

In this example the teacher applied a very common reward: attention. First she gave it in accordance with her theory that the child's misbehavior was a symptom of his need for attention: the child misbehaved and she gave him attention. Then she focused on behavior and gave the reward following desirable acts. When the child behaved well, she gave him attention. In this way the reward *followed* the behavior that the teacher wanted to increase. The result was that the good behavior increased, and the misbehavior decreased.

My point is that it was the behavior of the *teacher* that changed—the reinforcer (attention) stayed the same, but it was applied differently.

Parents who feel that the use of rewards is common sense often misuse them in just the way this teacher did. Another way that rewards are commonly misapplied involves a form of blackmail. For example, little George has been making a terrible racket with his new drum, obviously bent on becoming the new Buddy Rich:

Parent: "George, please be quiet. You're making a lot of noise and I have a headache."

George: (responds with a very loud, exceptionally original drum solo.)

Parent: "George, if you're quiet, I'll take you for a ride after while. But you have to be quiet."

George: (promptly drops his sticks and it gets so quiet you could hear a caterpillar dance.)

If you are like a lot of parents you will be asking, "What's wrong with that?" The parent wanted George to be quiet, so he offered a reward for quiet behavior. The answer to your question will be clear if you'll ask yourself what behavior preceded the parent's offer of a ride. The parent rewarded George for *making noise*, the very behavior she wanted to stop.

Remember that the principle of rewards states that behavior that is rewarded tends to be repeated. This means *any* behavior—not just desirable behavior—that is followed by a reward will tend to be repeated. True, George did get quiet, but he has learned that being noisy produces nice consequences.

Suppose for a moment that you are George. You want to reinforce your parent for giving you nice things—such as a ride in the car. You have found in the past that one thing that Mom finds rewarding is quiet, so you begin to make noise. Mom requests that you stop. That isn't the behavior you want, so you continue making noise. Finally she offers a ride in the car, so you turn down the volume sharply, thus rewarding her for offering you what you want.

I'm not suggesting that George thinks things through this way. It is more likely to happen unknowingly and automatically, as though he had a built-in radar for finding parental soft spots. Irrespective of why, the *fact* is that George is using rewards effectively in this episode and Mom isn't.

The principle of giving rewards requires that the reward *follow* desirable behavior. Mom's reward (the offer of a ride) followed noisiness, and no matter what Mom's intention was, no matter what she *thought* she was rewarding, George has been reinforced for playing noisily. He has learned that it pays to bug Mom.

You might protest that Mom didn't take George for a ride when he was noisy, she only offered to take him for a ride *if he would be quiet*. But being told you will get a reward is itself rewarding. Why else are people on quiz shows so happy when they are told they've won the jackpot? They know that it will be some time before they will actually receive the prize itself, but knowing they will get it is rewarding.

One of the things that makes the principle of rewarding behavior complicated is that your behavior may be rewarding when you don't intend it to be. A reinforcer is *anything* that increases the probability of a response.

Mom certainly did not intend for her offer of a ride to reward noise, but it did. I'm sorry about that, but it can't be helped. A reward is *anything* that increases the frequency of the behavior it follows.

It would have been better if, in the above example, the parent had ignored George's noisiness.* Then, when the child became quiet, Mom could have said, "My, you're behaving nicely. In fact, you've been so good, I wonder if you'd like to go for a ride later on?" This way the reinforcer (offer of a ride) follows the desired behavior, playing quietly. The chief reason parents have trouble getting children to behave well is that they respond only to the child's misbehavior. And they reward it, even though they may think they are punishing it.

Instead of waiting until George is making enough noise to waken a frozen mastodon, reward him when he is playing quietly. Instead of punishing Mary for getting her clothes dirty, reward her for keeping them clean. Instead of throwing up your hands when Picky Paul doesn't eat his spinach, offer him dessert when he *does* clean his plate.

One issue concerning positive reinforcement is that some parents feel it creates an expectation of being paid for things which children should do without being rewarded. A father once complained, "The next thing you know, he's going to hit me up for two bits every time he goes to the bathroom." But the truth of the matter is that all of us are continuously rewarding and punishing others. This is especially true with our children. The look on our face, the tone of our voice, our responses to their requests, are all inadvertent reinforcement.

The issue of bribes is simplified if parents are careful about what they communicate to their children. If their actions suggest that the child's behavior is so important to *them* that they are willing to pay him to behave the way they want, then this is obviously a bribe. The child's attention is also misdirected away from

---

*There are times when ignoring undesirable behavior is impractical or dangerous. In these cases corporal punishment is justified. Corporal punishment is discussed in chapter twelve.

what *he* thinks about his behavior to worrying about what his parents think. On the other hand, one of the basic facts of life is that adaptive behavior and success pay off (are reinforced). If a person succeeds, if he wins, if he achieves, there are rewards, monetary and otherwise. What parents should communicate is that they are attempting to make their home life-like. Since success pays off in the outside world, they will make sure adaptive behavior pays off while the child is living at home. Under these circumstances, even monetary rewards should not be regarded as bribes, but rather as data to help the child understand what the outside world is really like.

Some parents have been concerned about the problem of rewarding one child when another is not rewarded for the same behavior. If a child who is failing in school is rewarded for passing, what do you do about the other children who are already making passing grades? The answer is to tell the children that rewards are for growing and developing, and that a child cannot be rewarded for doing something he has already achieved. Siblings who are not being rewarded should be given the opportunity to grow in other ways, so that they might also receive rewards. For instance, a child having no problem in toilet training should not be rewarded for using the toilet, even though a sibling with problems *is* rewarded. But if the non-soiling child wished to raise his grades or take more responsibility around the house, he could be given a reward for this. Most children readily accept these circumstances, and can receive an impetus for additional growth in the process.

The principle that behaviors followed by rewards tend to be repeated implies that the reward must be *immediate*. Any delay—even several seconds—allows time for the child to do something else that you don't want to reinforce.

For example, suppose daughter Mary likes to play with the family pet, a beagle named Bullet. To children, one of the most intriguing things about a dog is its tail. They seem to like nothing better than to pull those tails—unless it is to pull on long floppy ears.

Anyway, Mary likes to pull on Bullet's various appendages, and Mom is afraid that she will injure the pet or that Bullet will finally snap at Mary to stop her from dragging him about the room by his ear.

Mom, having just read the first part of this chapter, decides to reward Mary for not pulling Bullet apart at the seams. She notices that Mary has been playing nicely with Bullet and decides to offer her a small piece of cookie.

But, on the way to deliver the goodie, Mom sees a coat that needs hanging up and returns it to the closet. Then she hands Mary the cookie, but by now Mary is pulling on the living room curtains.

What has Mom reinforced? You got it: curtain pulling.

"Well," you might say, "Mom could *explain* that the cookie is for not pulling on Bullet." She might, but it would do little good, especially with a three-year-old. Even with adults, rewards speak louder than words.

The only effective way of avoiding this problem is to reward *immediately*. That means, if possible, rewarding while the child is performing the desired act (playing nicely with Bullet) or, at the very least, rewarding her a second or two after she stops. And if, when you're on the way to deliver a reward, Mary's behavior changes to something undesirable, forget the reward.

The need for immediacy may seem to pose impossible problems in the use of rewards. But secondary reinforcers can often be delivered immediately.

You may smile and say, "It's nice to see you playing with Bullet without hurting him, Mary." You can deliver that kind of reward from across a crowded room, even if your hands are full of bread dough.

There will be times, however, when you won't feel very much like saying nice things. Sometimes even a wonderful, good-natured parent such as yourself is irritable or under the weather or preoccupied by some serious problem. On these occasions, you may find it difficult to praise, cuddle, or play with Junior, no matter how richly he deserves to be rewarded.

At times like these, poker chips can be a parent's best friend.

4

Token Rewards

Yes, poker chips. Or play money, or 3 x 5 index cards, or marbles, or pieces of construction paper, or postage stamps, or walnuts or buttons.

Poker chips are especially good because they come in different colors, they're durable, they aren't readily available to most children and they have absolutely no value, except to poker players.

No, I haven't been smoking any of those fancy cigarettes. The fact is that poker chips can be very helpful to a parent, especially if his children are young. This is because poker chips—or other objects without inherent value—can be used as reinforcers. The idea behind the poker chip is the principle that:

An Object Becomes Reinforcing If It Can Be Exchanged For Other Reinforcers

Take money, for example. A dollar bill is a germ-laden dirty piece of paper that any of us would jump into the gutter to retrieve. We get so used to the idea that money is a valuable commodity we forget that it's actually worthless: you can't eat it, sleep on it, or drink it; it won't keep you warm in the winter or shade you in the summer; it won't make you well when you're ill; you can't even blow your nose on it very well.

Money has value only because you can exchange it for things that do have value—like food, a place to sleep, a jacket, an air conditioner, medicine or a box of Kleenex.

Money is nothing more than a token that has value for goods and services. And it would make just as much sense to use poker chips for this purpose as it does paper with green ink on it.

Money is not the only kind of token that we use every day. Green stamps, food coupons, the famous rain check, the less famous hat check, bus tokens, poker chips, and IOU's all qualify. In fact, the ticket you use to get into a theater or a ball park is a *second-generation* token, since to get into the theater you have to exchange money (a token) for a ticket (also a token). Thus a ticket is a token you can buy with another token! Today, with money being transferred from bank to bank by computer, our whole economic system is starting to look like a number of crutches supported by a number of crutches.

The point is that tokens work as well as the real thing, even better. For example, if you hand an usher a theater ticket (a piece of paper that has absolutely no value outside of that theater) he'll show you to a seat. But if you hand him a banana, something that does have some value, he'll show you to the exit. Similarly, most car salesmen will be happy to give you a car in exchange for a check (a piece of paper that says you will give them other pieces of paper), but if you offer one a truck load of lemons, he'll get insulted. (Try it. They really get annoyed.) Since tokens are such a common part of our lives, why shouldn't parents use them with their children?

It's easy to set up a token system, or what psychologists call a token economy, in the home. First, choose some objects to act as tokens. The objects should be something not readily available to the child, nonperishable, light and small enough so that several can be carried in a pocket, and should come in several different colors.

The colors matter because, if there are two or more children, tokens can be a source of conflict; if Billy is only allowed to redeem blue poker chips and Mary is only allowed to redeem red ones, there will be less arguing over who took whose tokens.

Once you've selected a token, you need to assign it a value. Remember that tokens only have value if they can be exchanged for reinforcers; you would not continue working for your employer if your pay checks bounced.

In assigning a value to tokens, it's a good idea to make a list of things the child particularly likes and then determine the number of tokens necessary to obtain them. A list of items that can be exchanged for tokens might look something like this:

A trip to a favorite place (the zoo, the park, a recreation area), 12 tokens.

A period of time (say fifteen minutes) for which the child may stay up past his regular bedtime, 5 tokens.

A specified toy, such as a model plane, a Barbie doll, etc., 50 tokens.

It's also a good idea to assign a monetary value to the tokens, such as five cents each, so that the child can redeem his tokens as five cents each, for another token—cash. That will allow him the opportunity to spend his own money however he wishes. Be careful not to give the tokens greater monetary value than you will be able to afford. If you exchange them for a dollar each, for example, you may find yourself cutting down on the tokens you give in order to save yourself money. A nickel is probably a good place to start.

It's a good idea to write down the purchase price of each activity or object that can be exchanged for tokens. Give one copy to the child and save one for yourself; or, if you prefer, post the exchange list in some prominent place, (a playroom or bulletin board) where everyone can refer to it. There is no reason for the list to be exhaustive. Nobody said you should be able to buy a Cadillac with green stamps.

You will get a lot of questions: "What can I do to earn a token?" "What do I have to do to earn 20 tokens?"

You can make a list of chores and their values:

Mowing the lawn, 15 tokens
Making your bed without being reminded, 2 tokens
Washing dishes, 5 tokens
Making your own lunch, 1 token

Next, you have only to work out a system for redeeming the tokens. I recommend that you set aside a specific time, once a week, or at most, once a day, during which tokens can be used to purchase other items. This will free you from having to run a bank twenty-four hours a day.

Some children, like international governments, will try to outwit their competitors in the monetary market by changing the value of a token. It may be OK to reevaluate the franc in Paris or the yen in Tokyo, but right here in River City, a token is worth the same at the time of redemption that it was upon issuance. And no credit: no tokens for the promise of future virtues, only for present deeds. It's true that in God we trust, but in Junior, we can only hope.

While tokens can be exchanged for toys and other objects, the opposite does not hold. If ten tokens will buy a toy truck, the child may reason, a toy truck will buy ten tokens. The child must understand that all sales are final. Once he has selected the dump truck, that's what he has bought. If he later decides he'd rather have a jump rope, he'll have to buy it at the regular token price.

Tokens are an advantage in that they can be given at practically any time regardless of the mood of the parent. Unlike smiles, hugs and praise which should only be given when we can give them sincerely, tokens can be given out no matter what our mood.

For example, if Johnny has been a monster all morning but then behaves well, you may not be up to giving him a hug or telling him how pleased you are at his good behavior, but you *can* put a token in his hand.

Similarly, many parents give a weekly allowance in return for household chores, but this puts the reinforcer (the weekly pay check) far away from the desired behavior. Tokens allow you to reinforce the behavior *when it occurs*. They also encourage the child to be reponsible, since he has to save his tokens until the redemption period:

"Dad, I know I had more tokens than this. I must have lost some somewhere."

"Gee, that's too bad, Pat. I hope they turn up."

"But suppose they don't? I earned them, I should be able to use them. I may never find them. It isn't fair."

"Yes, I know it's hard to accept."

"You mean you will replace them?"

"No, I can't do that. But if I see them I'll let you know."

There are a couple of cautions in using tokens. Although they can be used at practically any age, they probably won't work very well with children under four years old. Then, in adolescence, some children will resent tokens; they'll feel it's too childish, and will want "real" money. When this happens, don't worry. It's only a transition from one token to another.

Some children, especially very young ones, will misuse tokens if given the opportunity. Parents may worry about the health of a child who regularly uses his tokens to buy sweets. You can anticipate problems of this sort and set restrictions ahead of time. For example, tokens might be redeemable for no more than one dessert a day.

Some parents may worry about the materialistic aspect of a token system, but tokens needn't be exchangeable only for *things*. In fact, tokens might be made redeemable only for activities: a movie, staying up 20 minutes past the regular bedtime, a trip into town, and so on.

About the only kind of reinforcer that I personally do not think a child should be able to buy with tokens is affection. Hugs and kisses should be given by the parent when he or she really feels like giving them. And that should be frequently during the day. If a child has to buy kisses from Mom and Dad, there's something wrong, and tokens are not the solution.

Tokens work suprisingly well, but you can't expect miracles. It would be great to say to your six-year-old, "OK, do four quadratic equations and I'll give you 40 tokens." He might be willing to comply, but he's just beginning to learn his numbers.

That leads us to another principle, which has to do with where you put your feet.

5

One Step At A Time

The longest journey, the Chinese say, begins with a single step. I might add that if you think of a journey as one great step, you'll probably never go anywhere.

Imagine, for example, that you want to go to the Grand Canyon. You can't do it. Nobody can "just go" to the Grand Canyon, not even Evil Knievel. What you *can* do is get into your car and drive along the road out of town, through various states (unless you live in Arizona), and gradually make your way to your destination. You might stop along the way, eat, buy gas, etc. You see that going to the Grand Canyon means performing a number of small acts which taken together, will get you where you want to go. (These steps could, of course, be broken down still further: getting into the car, starting it, backing out of the driveway, etc.)

Similarly, if you simply wait for your child to solve quadratic equations, thinking that all you have to do is reward him when he reaches that destination, your M&M's are apt to melt in your hand, not in his mouth. And if the animal trainer waited until his elephant got on top of a ball and rolled it around the floor, the animal would starve for lack of peanuts.

The point is that the behavior you would like to see in your child may be completely non-existent. It may be too complicated, as in taking a trip or solving quadratic equations. Or it may be something which, for lack of past rewards, has never become an established behavior, such as studying. Regardless of *why* the desired behavior rarely or never occurs, it makes little sense to stand over the child, rewards or tokens in hand, waiting to give praise or sing the Hallelujah Chorus when the desired act occurs.

Even the most complicated behavior, however, can be broken down into small steps, and when you examine the steps necessary to perform a given act, you will see that your son or daughter already performs some of them. All you need do is start with what the child *can do* and follow principle five:

Improvements That Are Rewarded Will Lead To Further Improvements.

This principle may seem absurd. It may seem unjust, or softheaded. "Does this mean," you might ask, "that if Jerry is getting F's we should praise him for bringing home a D?" The answer is an emphatic *yes*!

Look, even a student who hates school and who boasts of his terrible grades will occasionally, if unintentionally, bring home a report card or a homework assignment or a test that has a grade higher than F. It may only be an F +. But if that F + is rewarded, it will lead to more F + grades. Then, perhaps quite by accident, there will be an occasional D −. If that is rewarded, there will be more D − grades, which will lead to a D +, which will lead to a C −, and so on. As the Alaskans say, Nome wasn't built in a day.

There are limits, of course. A retarded child is not apt to reach Einsteinian levels of performance. But if you concentrate on what the child can do now and reward improvements, *however slight,* then the child can develop his maximum potential.

Perhaps some examples will help to illustrate this principle. We might begin by looking at how it was discovered by B.F. Skinner.

During the early stages of World War II, three psychologists, B.F. Skinner, James Holland, and Keller Breland were sitting in a laboratory in a Minneapolis grain elevator. They were waiting for a telegram from Washington, D.C. which would tell them whether or not their request for a government research grant had been approved. It was summer and open windows were the most common form of air conditioning.

Skinner noticed a pigeon perched on a window sill. Having nothing better to do, he grabbed a handful of grain and approached this feathered foe of statues. What could he get this pigeon to do if he took things one step at a time? He first gave the bird a piece of grain for facing the inside of the room, but nothing if it looked away. Soon the pigeon was facing forward like a guard at Buckingham Palace. Reinforcement for *looking* was then discontinued, and the pigeon had to take a step toward the inside of the room in order to get his grain. After this behavior was firmly established, he was required to take two steps, then three, then four, etc., before being rewarded. In a few minutes Skinner had trained a pigeon to enter the room and go anywhere within it, as his mentor desired.

Skinner and other psychologists have been able to teach pigeons to turn around in circles, to peck a key, and do all sorts of things that pigeons seldom do. Skinner even taught one pair of pigeons to play ping pong!

I am not saying that your children are nothing more than featherless pigeons. But the principle of rewarding improvements works as well for people learning very complex skills as it does for pigeons and other animals learning simple tasks.

Suppose, for example, that your twelve-year-old Bernie is shy around strangers. Up to a certain age, many people find shyness in a child cute. But there is a point at which extreme shyness interferes with a child's normal functioning.

Like it or not, meeting new people is a part of living in society, and living in fear of such experiences will severely limit a person's chances of happiness and success. Consider, for example, how difficult it would be to be a salesman, work in a store, own a business or practice a profession if one were extremely shy.

What can you do to help the child overcome his shyness?

Begin by asking yourself what it means to be *not* shy, and set this as your goal. What would you like the child to be able to do without feeling uncomfortable? This is extremely important since it is not possible to reward improvements unless you know what your goal is. Okay, you decide that, for his age a child should be able to greet people he does not know at the door, introduce himself and ask their names, and stay with them until the person whom they have come to visit arrives.

The next step is to decide what the child already can do without discomfort. Let's say that he can watch from a distance as someone else answers the door. The next step would be to reward him for getting closer to the door, for viewing the greeting process from a closer point.

A common mistake at times like this is to get impatient and yank the child over to the door or even make him participate in the greeting process. Sometimes this gets the job done, though at considerable expense to the child. But sometimes it makes matters worse, so that the child stays even farther away than before. He might, for example, sneak out of the back door when he hears or sees visitors approaching. Be patient and remember that if you reward improvements, further improvements are certain to come.

In this way you gradually reward the child for getting closer and closer, never *requiring* him to move forward, but rewarding him for whatever progress he makes. (Incidentally, it would speed things up if you could arrange to have visitors frequently; if the opportunity to reward improvements occurs only once a month, it would take forever to get the final desired behavior.)

After a time, Bernie is quite willing to come to the door with you or some other member of the family to greet visitors. By now, you have the problem practically licked.

Whoever greets the visitors should always make a point of saying, "This is my son, Bernie." It is not necessary to prod Bernie into saying hello—remember that you are to reward improvements as they occur, not force them to occur. Besides, Bernie knows that people usually say hello in such situations, and he will when he's ready. When he does, be sure to give him a big smile, show him that you're proud of him or otherwise satisfy his own particular reward appetite. If you have adopted a token system, you might just put a token in his hand unobtrusively.

The next step is for Bernie to begin greeting people himself. At first you might reward him for simply saying hello and nothing else. Once he seems comfortable with that, you should reward him for introducing himself: "Hello, I'm Bernie Smith."

Once a new behavior is well established, you reward further improvements. When Bernie is handling things at the door very well, you might stand back from the doorway a bit so that he has the show to himself. (By this time he will probably be getting a kick out of the performance.) Gradually you will find that you can rely on Bernie to answer the door entirely on his own.

Once Bernie has mastered the art of greeting visitors, you will probably find that he is less shy in other situations. If there are other areas of shyness that should be overcome, you can work on those in a similar step by step manner.

Although the process of building toward a particular behavior seems complicated, there are really only a few simple steps: decide what behavior you want to occur and reward improvements toward that goal.

Once a behavior is established, reward any improvement. Once that improved behavior is established, look again for improvement.

Parents sometimes object to this procedure. Faced with a problem like Bernie's they may say, "Oh, he'll outgrow it." And he may outgrow it—although outgrowing it means the successive improvements will be rewarded naturally. The trouble with the grow-out-of-it theory is that, first he may not outgrow it; in fact, it could get worse. Secondly, outgrowing a problem such as this takes considerably longer than systematically rewarding improvements. Thirdly, a problem of this sort can become a source of conflict, pulling the parents and the child away from each other.

Childhood fears are often a source of disruption in a family, so examples of rewarding improvements to overcome a problem of this sort may be helpful.

Howie was a fifteen-year-old mentally retarded boy who was terrified of elevators. He did not seem to mind high places or small, closed places, but at the sight of an elevator, he trembled until each knee smote one against the other. In some cases he had stomach cramps so painful he would grab his midsection and fall to his knees. To help him overcome this fear, we began with what he could do—peer at an elevator from around a corner. When he did so he was praised and given a pat on the back.

Once Howie was able to watch the elevator without feeling uneasy, he was asked to come out from around the corner and stand in the hallway. He would come out into the hall and stand against the wall opposite the elevator, about ten feet away from it. He would look at the elevator and then retreat behind the corner. He was rewarded each time he came out into the hall and looked at the elevator, but he was no longer rewarded for peering at it from around the corner.

Next, he was rewarded for taking a step toward the elevator. He was rewarded for standing nine feet away, then he had to be within eight feet to be rewarded, then seven, then six and so on until he was able to touch the elevator door. Next he was asked to touch the inside of the elevator, then to touch deeper inside the elevator, then to stand inside of it.

As he became comfortable with each new behavior, the next small step was required of him and he was reinforced for it until he was comfortable with that behavior. Finally he was able to stand in the elevator while the door was closed one inch and then quickly reopened. Then the door was closed two inches and he was rewarded, then three inches and so on until he was able to take an elevator ride with a minimum of discomfort.

In this case, the act of riding an elevator was broken down into about fifty separate steps, each one a little closer to the final appropriate behavior. The total process took only eight sessions of thirty minutes each despite the fact that this fear had existed for as long as the boy or his parents could remember.

I don't want to leave you with the impression that rewarding improvements in behavior applies only to problems like shyness and fear of elevators. Actually, it's a principle that applies to developing any new behavior or one that occurs so seldom it would be difficult to try to increase it by rewarding it.

For example, the F student mentioned earlier could be rewarded for slight improvements with much better results than parents would get by punishing his poor performance or by offering a reward for straight A's. The child who never cleans his room could at first be rewarded when he spontaneously puts away his dirty underwear. Instead of lecturing and carrying on about what the child doesn't do, focus on what he does do and reward improvement.

"Okay," I hear you saying, "I've got the kid riding the elevator or answering the door or making good grades or going to the bathroom by himself or playing nicely with his brothers and sisters. But I can't keep running after him with a bag of M&M's or tokens the rest of my life. This business of rewarding desired behavior and rewarding improvements to get desired behavior is dandy so long as I can be there, but I can't always be there. Won't the child revert to his old ways once I stop rewarding him every time he does something?"

Fortunately, the answer is no. Not if you understand when less is more.

6

When Less Is More

Ever go to Nevada? In Las Vegas, Reno, Lake Tahoe, or for that matter, just about any town in Nevada, you'll find people with slightly glazed eyes and fast hands standing in front of slot machines as if hypnotized. You may have even been one of those zombies yourself.

The reward for feeding coins to these one-armed bandits seems obvious: money, that very powerful token that we all love so dearly. But most people lose far more money than they win. Businessmen in ties, cowboys in blue jeans, housewives with their hair in curlers, and the ubiquitous little old lady in tennis shoes stand there, hour after hour, losing quarter after quarter after quarter.

Why? When the odds are obviously stacked against them, why do these people throw their money away? They are getting fewer rewards from the machine than they are giving it, so why don't they quit? Part of the answer is that sometimes less is more. The people who run gambling halls have learned principle six which says that:

Once a Behavior is Established, It Can Be Maintained with Occasional Rewards

All the casino has to do is get you to try your luck. They do this by adapting the slot machines so that every time someone wins a few quarters, a light on the machine flashes on and off, a bell rings, and coins are dropped a few at a time into a metal tray. The lights and ringing bells attract your attention and the ca-ching, ca-ching of the money falling into the tray makes you drool. You try it. Just one quarter—for the fun of it. Lights are flashing, bells are ringing, and coins are ca-chinging all around you and these rewards actually reward *you* for putting in that first coin. So you try another quarter. Then another. Then another. Finally, just as you're about to walk away, you *win*.

And you're hooked. The machine only rewards you occasionally, but once the behavior is established, it can be maintained at a high rate with occasional reinforcement. In fact, strange as it may sound, research consistently shows that rewarding only occasionally can have more lasting effects on behavior than rewarding a response every time it occurs. This is why people stick at those slot machines and why the duffer who hits only two or three good shots in a round of golf keeps on playing.

To establish a behavior, you usually have to reward frequently. But once the person responds appropriately, you will get even better (more lasting) results by rewarding his behavior occasionally. The trick is to go gradually from constant or frequent reinforcement to occasional reinforcement. An example may help:

Seven-year-old Mary has a habit of throwing her clothes wherever she happens to be when she takes them off. She comes in the door, and the coat goes on the floor. She takes off her school clothes in the bedroom so that's where you'll find them—on the bedroom floor.

Mrs. Jones, her mother, tried explaining to her that a girl of her age should put her clothes away. Mary promises to do better, but there is only a short-lived improvement, then back to the old style (or sty, I should say). Mom explains again and tells her again how clothes that aren't hung up get dirty and have to be washed more often, how clothes left on the floor can be a hazard since someone could trip on them. No results.

Mom threatens to take drastic measures if Mary doesn't stop leaving clothes around; there is another temporary improvement, then a relapse. The situation degenerates into more threats, loud voices, punishment, crying, and more clothes on the floor.

Finally, just as she is seriously considering putting Mary up for adoption, Mrs. Jones comes across this marvelous book. She reads the first four chapters, and instead of going on with the adoption plan, decides to go to work on Mary's dropsy problem. She says nothing more to Mary about hanging up clothes, but watches Mary closely and when her jacket falls accidentally on the sofa instead of landing on the floor, Mom says, "Well, that's much better, Mary. I appreciate your keeping the jacket off the floor." Mary hardly notices as she runs into the bedroom to change her clothes which she leaves all over the floor. Mom persists. She knows that if she rewards improvements, she will reach her goal.

One day Mrs. Jones notices that Mary has put some of her clothes on the bed instead of on the floor. She quickly rewards this by saying, "Mary, I noticed you put some of your clothes on the bed. That's very nice. Would you like some cookies before you go out to play?" And so it goes, Mom keeps rewarding improvements and the improvements keep coming. In a few weeks, the problem is licked. Mary nearly always puts her clothes away; sometimes she's a little messy about it, not getting the clothes on the hangers neatly, but her behavior is pretty good for a seven-year-old and Mom is satisfied.

"But what will happen," Mrs. Jones worries, "if I stop rewarding Mary for putting her clothes away? Do I *always* have to stand ready to praise or offer cookies and milk?"

In desperation Mrs. Jones searches the world and its literature. She wanders from guru to guru, but finally she comes back to these splendiferous pages, the source of truly sage advice. She is not disappointed. Mrs. Jones, here is what you should do: Mary's behavior is well established. Begin tapering off on the rewards very slowly. Right now you are rewarding Mary nearly every time she puts her clothes away. Skip the reinforcer on one occasion. If Mary says anything, ("Hey, didn't you notice I put my clothes away?") be sure to assure her that you did notice and you appreciate her efforts. Reward the next four or five instances of the desired behavior and then skip another reinforcer. Gradually reduce the reinforcement to one every two or three responses, then once every four or five, and so on, until you are only rewarding occasionally, or when Mary does a particularly good job of putting her clothes away neatly.

Don't get too stingy with the rewards, and if there is a re-occurrence of her past sloppiness, reward her good behavior more often.

Actually, the principle of occasional reinforcement is not a new one. Once a behavior is established, what you need to reward is *persistence* in that behavior. You begin by rewarding small amounts of persistence, then gradually increase the degree of persistence needed to get a reward. Occasional rewards can have an additional benefit. They will not only maintain a behavior, but they will often increase its occurrence. A child who has been rewarded regularly for practicing at the piano for thirty minutes a day may begin practicing for longer periods as the number of rewards diminishes. I don't guarantee these bonus improvements in behavior, but they will sometimes be a pleasant surprise.

Luckily, most desirable behaviors are reinforced occasionally even outside of the home. People say thanks. They smile, they offer to buy you a cup of coffee or take you to a movie, they shake your hand, they praise you. This sort of reinforcement is often too infrequent to establish a behavior, but once a behavior is established, the occasional rewards will maintain it. And, best of all, adaptive behavior, whether it be neatness, losing weight, or whatever, is often its own reward. It really is nice to be able to find your own socks in what was formerly chaos or to get positive vibes from the opposite sex rather than the subtle "my, aren't you fat" glances.

There are, however, a couple of cautions to keep in mind in moving toward occasional reinforcement. As I have already pointed out, it is important to decrease the reward frequency gradually, and if the behavior begins to drop off, return to the previous level of reward frequency.

Another caution has to do with the distinction between reinforcement and payment. If you set up a token system and agree to pay one token each time Mary hangs up her coat or puts away her clothes, you cannot gradually reduce the payment just because she does the work. After all, how would you feel if your boss came in one day and said, "Congratulations! You've been doing so well, we've decided to reduce your pay." A contract is a contract. Stick by it.

So far, I've been telling you about how to reward desirable behaviors. Concentrating on rewarding Mary for putting her clothes away will work better in the long run than screaming at her for *not* putting her clothes away. Of course, it also helps if the parents are perfect.

7

Do As I Do. Then You'll Be Perfect, Too

We are fond of saying that experience is the best teacher, that we learn by doing. But much learning takes place by observing others, not by direct experience. If you think about this a moment, you'll see that it's true; but observational learning is so natural, so common, that we tend to take it for granted. We think we're teaching someone only when we instruct, praise, or criticize their performance. But Emerson's reminder that "What you are thunders so loudly I cannot hear what you are saying," is certainly true in the parent-child relationship. How we behave may do as much or more than anything else to shape our children's character and behavior. They'll likely not stick with a difficult task unless they've observed perseverance. They probably won't even strive to achieve unless they've seen someone succeed (a real problem for ghetto children). They won't develop a conscience unless they see morality at home. And we increase the probability that they will smoke or perform other unhealthy acts if we commit them ourselves. We already know that behavior that is rewarded tends to be repeated, but modeling can help to guarantee that certain behaviors will or will not occur in the first place.

Parents of handicapped children come to appreciate the importance of modeling very quickly. The deaf child cannot imitate sounds he cannot hear, so teaching him to speak requires special effort. Similarly, the blind child cannot observe much of what goes on around him, so he has little opportunity to imitate the behavior of others. Probably the greatest handicap that blind or deaf children face is this inability to learn vicariously from the behavior of others. It is the impaired input from their environment that hurts them most, not the limits on what they can do.

Children are very astute observers. They notice what other people do and they notice the payoffs that behavior gets. When they like these results, they imitate the behavior. This brilliant observation is summarized by the monkey principle:

Behavior That Is Rewarded in Others Tends To Be Imitated

This "monkey see, monkey do" principle has been demonstrated in animals as well as people. For example, a monkey was trained to open a box to get a raisin. Other monkeys watched this demonstration and were given a chance at a similar problem. In most cases the monkeys quickly opened the box and got the raisin, whereas monkeys who hadn't had the chance to watch the solution were not so quick. Studies with children yield similar results, supporting the suspicion of some adults that children are really little monkeys.

In one study, children played with toys while an adult hit a large BoBo doll. When these children had an opportunity to play with the doll, they not only played with it, they did the same kinds of things that the adult had done: they sat on it, kicked it, tossed it in the air and, while doing so, made the same kinds of comments the adult had made.

Many undesirable behaviors get their start in just this way. For example, suppose that Penny sees another child take a toy away from a playmate. The playmate is smaller and unable to do much about the theft, except cry. Meanwhile, the thief is effecting a clean getaway. Parental lectures about sharing, recognizing ownership and the rights of others are about as worthless as a Slobbovian nickel at today's inflation rate. What counts is that pushing and taking the toy works! Penny sees this, and imitates it by approaching the thief (who is smaller than Penny) and yanking the toy away from *her*. As I said before, behavior that is rewarded in others will tend to be imitated.

Oddly enough, children often pick up their worst habits by imitating their parents. If Mom is afraid of thunder and lightning, little Susie may run and hide every time the clouds get dark. When Dad gets angry, he curses like a graffiti crazed mariner. But he is admired and respected. To be rewarded—with power and respect and admiration—one must obviously behave as Dad behaves. So when Evan hits his thumb with his toy hammer, his next dozen sentences sound like the prose on a bathroom wall. If Mom gets her way when she weeps, Dotty will most certainly give weeping a fair number of honest tries.

Habits such as smoking and other forms of drug abuse, overeating, slovenliness and physical aggression are usually learned by observing and imitating adults, especially parents. When these behaviors are tried, the child is reinforced by feeling very adult and by the awe he or she inspires in his peers. "Wow," a child may say, "Mike smokes cigarettes!" The possibility of getting lung cancer in thirty years means nothing, and even if nausea hits it may not be enough to outweigh the prestige the behavior brings.

Not suprisingly, many adult problems have their roots in childhood—not so much in the sense of psychological traumas, but in the habits people acquire by imitating their parents. Adults who have a history of child abuse, for example, are often found to be people who were beaten severely by their parents when they were children. And wife beaters often come from families in which violence, including wife beating, was part of the daily routine.

Right about now, you may be thinking that you can forget much of what we said earlier about rewards and tokens. Since children imitate their parents, all you need do is behave the way you want your child to behave. Be perfect, and have perfect children. Not so. The problem is that there is a distinction between learning a skill and performing it. If a child of, say, nine observes someone opening a combination lock, he will probably be "able" to open it himself. He will know how to open it, without your giving him praise or tokens. But whether he *will* open it depends upon other influences—including rewards and punishment.

For example, if you use good table manners yourself, then your child will learn these manners. But sometimes he will talk with his mouth full or throw food across the table at his brother. He does these things not (God forbid) because he has seen you doing them, but because there are rewards for doing them. When one has something important to say, it is rewarding to say it right away, even if it means violating the rules of etiquette. And when your brother flashes a nasty look or says something unkind, it is rewarding to throw a lima bean at him. Although good table manners have been learned—in the sense that the child knows what they are and is capable of using them—they may not always be *performed*. This is when rewards and punishment become important.

The principle of imitation says that behavior that is rewarded in others will be imitated. Fred sees his older brother being praised for giving the pet dog a bath. He imitates that behavior by giving the canary a bath. The results are not the same: brother was praised, but Fred is punished. Fred gives up his plans to be a vet. Or Priscilla watches her brother do somersaults on the front yard and notices how happy his feats make her mother. She proceeds to do somersaults only to be criticized for being "unladylike." Priscilla gives up on gymnastics.

Another example: Harry gets into a fight with the school bully and wins. All the other kids praise him and want to be his pal. Richard can't wait to imitate Harry. He picks a fight with the bully, but gets broken in more places than the Ten Commandments. Not only does Richard suffer the bumps and bruises of the losing end of a fight, but the other kids laugh at him and tease him. Richard becomes a pacifist.

The point I'm trying to make is that the principle of imitation does not over-rule the other principles we have covered. Instead, it works with those principles. Behavior that is rewarded in others will be imitated, but whether the behavior persists depends upon what happens next. If Fred had washed the dog, instead of the canary, he might have been praised and would have repeated his efforts later. If Priscilla's somersaults had gotten cheers from her mother instead of boos, she might have gone on to dancing fame as the next generation's partner for Fred Astaire. If Richard had won the fight with the bully, he might have become a Kung-Fu freak.

I'm not saying that a child's whole life and happiness depend upon the outcome of a single event. Far from it. All I'm saying is that children will imitate an act if they have reason to believe it will have good results, but from then on their own experiences, especially if there is a consistent theme, will determine whether the act becomes a habit or evaporates like the foggy, foggy dew.

Given that limitation, it is important for parents to try to provide a good example for their children. Dorothy Law Nolte summarized my point nicely:

Children Learn What They Live

If a child lives with criticism, He learns to condemn.

If a child lives with hostility, He learns to fight.

If a child lives with ridicule, He learns to be shy.

If a child lives with shame, He learns to feel guilty.

If a child lives with tolerance, He learns to be patient.

If a child lives with encouragement, He learns confidence.

If a child lives with praise, He learns to appreciate.

If a child lives with fairness, He learns justice.

If a child lives with security, He learns to have faith.

If a child lives with approval, He learns to like himself.

If a child lives with acceptance and friendship, He learns to find love in the world.

The principle of imitation will go a long way in developing desirable behaviors. If, however, you are faced with a well-established *unwanted* behavior, the first thing to do is follow the path of the brontosaurus.

Lesson From A Brontosaurus

The brontosaurus was a very large, powerful dinosaur that roamed the earth millions of years before we *Homo sapiens* ever appeared. It was a vegetarian so it didn't have any trouble finding food in the humid, plant-rich earth that was its home, and it had few enemies. But despite all these good points, the last brontosaurus died millions of years ago. You might say that it died of non-reinforcement. What happened was that the earth changed and the brontosaurus didn't. The characteristics and behavioral patterns that made it flourish in one period worked against it in another.

Presumably, this same scenario has been followed a thousand times since life first crawled out of the ooze millions of years ago. Some creatures thrive in a particular environment while others move on to other areas or die out. The survivors have physical or behavioral characteristics that are rewarded by the environment; the losers don't.

If the environment changes slowly, sometimes successive generations of a species will get smaller and smaller, or larger and larger, or will make some other change dictated by the environment. But one way or another, the characteristics or habits of a species that are not rewarded—that do not help the creature to survive—die out. The changes that the environment required of the brontosaurus and other dinosaurs were too great and the entire species became extinct.

Behavior evolves in much the same way that a species does. It changes to meet the demands of the environment, and behaviors that are not rewarded—that do not help the individual get along in that environment—die out. Behavior, like the brontosaurus, can be made extinct. The brontosaurus principle states that:

Behavior That Consistently Goes Unrewarded *Will Disappear*

Psychologists, perhaps in memory of the brontosaurus, like to say the behavior has been extinguished.

As you can see, this principle is the complement of the principle that behavior that is rewarded tends to be repeated. But it is important to note the word "consistently" in principle eight. If you want to get rid of some annoying behavior, often the easiest way to do so is to make sure that you *never* reward it. The trouble is that if you reward the behavior once in a while, you are using occasional reinforcement. As you recall from chapter six, occasional reinforcement maintains behavior better than constant reinforcement.

Your *intention* may be to get rid of some habit, but sometimes you give in or you smile without thinking. Whether you intended to or not, you have strengthened the very behavior you want to do away with! To extinguish or get rid of an undesirable behavior, you must not reward it *at all*.

The difference between occasional reinforcement and non-reinforcement is usually not appreciated by parents. They see the occasional reward as a harmless exception to a rule. You may have told Jane a million times not to exaggerate. But today, Jane exaggerated and said something very funny and you couldn't help laughing. Now you've become your own worst enemy, rewarding her for exaggerating. If you do this with any regularity, even though it is only "now and then," Jane's habit of exaggerating will become solidly entrenched.

If you will focus on your own behavior, you probably will discover that you are more inconsistent than you realize. You make rules, but sometimes when they are broken you look the other way, or you may even laugh or approve. You may, for example, tell Billy that he should not fight. When Billy comes home with a black eye the size of a frisbee, Dad gives him a lecture on the value of cooperation, the importance of getting along and of settling differences peacefully. But after this U.N. speech, Dad walks over to Mom, smiles and says, "Did you see the size of that shiner! He's some boy!" Smiles of approval and comments of this sort—even though not directed to Billy—can be extremely rewarding. This can even overrule the effect of a spanking.

Another common example of how occasional rewards unintentionally strengthen unwanted behavior can be seen in any supermarket on Saturday. Look for a parent who is shopping with a young child. When you see a child who is saying "Buy me this," or "Daddy, I want a . . . ," watch carefully. (You may see yourself in this more easily than someone else.) Typically the parent says, "No, you can't have that; you have plenty of candy (toys, cereal, etc.) at home." Sometimes the parent will say, "No, I'm not buying you anything today, so don't ask." But the child continues to ask with the rhythm of an Indian medicine man chanting over the sick: "Buy me this, buy me this, buy me this, buy me this. . . ." The parent tries to ignore the drone but it continues. Next Mom or Dad gets angry and threatens, or spanks the child, but he persists. Often the parent relents at this point, as much out of regard for the eardrums of his fellow shoppers as for his own peace of mind. Sometimes the parent ignores the crying, but as the sobs fade away, that never ending chant begins again, falteringly at first, then stronger, more confidently, more demandingly than before: "Buy me this, buy me this, buy me this. . . ." Eventually, the parent succumbs, tired, irritable, headachy and hopelessly defeated.

What the parent has done in the above example is to reward not only the "buy me this" behavior, but the child's persistence as well. Remember that in the last chapter we saw that occasional reinforcement maintained behavior very well because it was actually rewarding the child for persisting in the behavior. But the principles of behavior are completely impartial: they are not on the parent's side, and if the parent ignores them, they will work against him as readily as they will work for him. So to extinguish a behavior, to make it as rare as the brontosaurus, the parent must *consistently* avoid rewarding it, no matter what the costs. Do not fall into the trap of occasionally giving in as the parent did in the grocery store.

The problem of occasionally rewarding unwanted behavior is such a common one that another example is warranted.

Brian is a picky eater. (You may recognize him already.) Let's look in on Brian at mealtime:

Brian: (picks at the green beans on his otherwise clean plate)

Mom: Come on Brian, eat your beans, they're good for you.

Brian: (no response, except to push some of the beans around with his fork)

Mom: Don't you want to grow up to be big and strong?

Brian: (same behavior)

Mom: Now Brian, I am not having this. EAT YOUR BEANS!

Brian: Aw, Mom, you know I hate green beans. They taste like plastic.

Mom: Brian, if you don't eat your beans, you won't get any dessert. (Mom spears some of the beans with a fork and points the fork toward Brian's mouth)

Brian: (grimaces and turns away)

Mom: (exasperated) Oh, all right, starve: see if I care. You're absolutely the worst child I've ever seen. (Mother now gets the dessert and gives it to Brian) Well, (turning toward Dad) if I didn't give him dessert he wouldn't get enough to eat. It's practically the only thing he'll eat. I don't know what to do with that boy.

Now, I can hear some of you saying, "I'd know what to do with him! I'd knock him across the room." There is a place for corporal punishment, as you will see in a later chapter, but the problem here is that Mom is actually rewarding the very behavior she wants to get rid of. Not only that, she is using the occasional reinforcement that makes the behavior persistent. In this case Brian's persistent refusal to eat his beans was rewarded by (1) his not having to eat them (they taste like plastic), (2) getting dessert, and (3) the opportunity to gain extra attention and otherwise manipulate Mom (which may be the most reinforcing component of all).

If you are going to give in, do so immediately. You will be rewarding the undesired behavior, but at least you won't be rewarding persistence in the undesired behavior.

Perhaps now we should look at some illustrations of how the principle of non-reward can be applied by a parent. A common problem for parents is getting their children to go to bed on time and stay there. Some kids cry and whine when bedtime comes. Some beg to stay up for just a few more minutes. Others will come up with absolutely ingenious excuses for being granted another half hour of wakefulness. "Oh, I just remembered," one will say, "I forgot to do my math homework!" Another, knowing how pleased you are by her interest in music says, "Couldn't I just stay up to practice my piano for a little while? Please." To a mother hoping her little girl will become a female Van Cliburn, this is a hard request to refuse.

Five-year-old Laura's tactic was to go to bed and then call her parents to her. She wouldn't sleep more than four hours at a time. And Mom had to be right there with her or Laura would create a ruckus. (And little Laura *knew* how to create a ruckus.) The result was that Laura's mother spent most of the night at Laura's side. Laura could take a nap the next day, but that wasn't always possible for Mom. To say that Laura's parents were unhappy about this situation is like saying that Custer didn't appreciate Sitting Bull's idea of a party.

They tried every trick they could think of to get Laura to go to sleep. They reasoned with her, criticized her, threatened her, spanked her. Nothing worked. What had not occurred to them was that they were rewarding Laura's mis-behavior by giving her attention. (Remember, in addition to the attention itself, controlling one's parents can also be a real gas to most kids.)

Laura's parents sought professional help. They were advised to stop rewarding the unwanted behavior. At 8:00 p.m. Laura was put to bed, the light was turned off and she was told affectionately, "We'll see you in the morning." Period. No discussion. The door was latched from the outside so that Laura could not come out. No matter what Laura did, the parents did not open that door until 7:00 a.m.

On the first night, Laura protested vigorously for an hour and a half. Next night she gave up after thirteen minutes and on the third night she quit after five minutes. After that Laura objected only a few times and then only for short periods. The parents did not need to reason or threaten or punish or plead. All they had to do was stop rewarding the unwanted behavior. All they had to do was remember the brontosaurus.

When parents decide to remove all reinforcers for a behavior, and thereby extinguish that behavior, they will be faced with a couple of problems. These need not be a hindrance as long as parents know they're coming.

First, when a behavior is well established and the parents decide to stop rewarding it, there is likely to be a temporary *increase* in the behavior. It is as though the child can't believe the rewards are being held back. If two-year-old Freddie usually gets picked up and cuddled when he has tantrums, then *not* picking him up and cuddling him will produce an initial increase in tantrum behavior. And if the behavior has been rewarded occasionally rather than every time, it will take longer to extinguish: after all, by rewarding occasionally you have taught him that it pays to be persistent, so he will persist. Finally, however, you will win if you will just be consistent and not reward, *not ever*.

The second problem comes later. Just when the problem seems to be licked, just when you're about to drink a toast to youself, the behavior will re-occur. "Hey," you will say, "that's not fair. I didn't reinforce that behavior." This automatic, unrewarded re-occurrence of a behavior is called "spontaneous re-covery." It is a common occurrence and will not cause any problems as long as the parents don't panic. Continue with your commitment to avoid reinforcing, and the behavior will quickly disappear. If, however, you relent at this time, the behavior will quickly return to its old level and you will have to extinguish it all over again.

Withholding rewards for undesirable behaviors is a very handy way of getting rid of annoying habits. It works beautifully, though it requires some perseverance. The use of this procedure, however, rests on one important assumption: that the reinforcers maintaining the behavior are under the control of the parents. It works very well when the rewards have been coming from Mom and Dad, since they have only to stop giving the rewards.

But what if the behavior is intrinsically reinforcing—as in sniffing glue, watching TV for hours on end, smearing paint on the walls? What if the rewards come from other people—a teacher, relative, or friend of the family or from the child's classmates?

If Johnny shows off in class it's more likely because of the attention it brings from his peers than because of anything you do. If Mary talks on the phone for hours, it's more likely because of the fun in talking to her friends than because of the negative attention she gets from you. Withholding reinforcement is a technique that works only if the parent has control over the rewards that maintain the behavior. As the child gets older, more and more of his reinforcers come from people other than the parents. It's at this point that parents would often like to stop the whole ball game, throw up their hands and call "Time out!"

And that's what I suggest.

9

Time Out

You know now that to increase desirable behavior, you must reward it; to get rid of undesirable behavior, you must avoid rewarding it. But you are not the only source of rewards in the world. And sometimes the environment—meaning other people or objects around the child—rewards behavior that you would rather not have rewarded. Yet often it is difficult to remove the reinforcers, since they come from other people or things.

Mom and Dad are relaxing in the living room, watching the news on TV. Five-year-old Bobby is meandering about the room obviously bored stiff. Over to the TV set he goes, and the next thing you know, instead of Walter Cronkite reporting on the tax rebate, you're watching Captain Kirk and Mr. Spock get the Star Ship Enterprise out of another inter-galactic mess.

"Turn it back to the news, Bobby." Bobby responds by turning the channel selector further away from Walter and your tax money and into the realm of a Mission Impossible. What do Mom and Dad do now? They are not rewarding their child for stealing their TV show. How can parents escape this frustrating situation? Can they have Bobby recalled by the factory? No, but they can call Time Out.

In Time Out, instead of removing the reinforcers, you remove the child. This is very useful when a child is being rewarded for misbehaving in a particular situation.

In ice hockey, any player who commits a foul is sent to a penalty box for a specified period. Your parents may have said to you when you were a child (I hope not recently), "If you can't play quietly in the house, you'll have to go outside" or, "If you don't use good manners at the dinner table, you'll have to leave." You may have had a teacher in elementary school who used Time Out. He may have made you stand in the hall, or go to the cloak room when you misbehaved in class. All of these are ways of using Time Out, though not in its ideal form.

To a psychologist, Time Out is shorthand for "time out from reinforcement." As I suggested above, it means that when a child misbehaves in a situation, you remove him from that situation for a specified period. It is based upon the principle that:

Behavior That Results in Removal From a Rewarding Situation Tends To Be Avoided

In the example above, Bobby's channel changing is probably rewarded by the fact that he gets more fun out of watching the pointy-eared Spock than he does from listening to a white haired guy "named Crank Knock or something," talk about taxes. Of course, the reinforcer for his rude behavior could be something else—the attention he gets from his parents, for example. It really doesn't matter: the behavior is undesirable and should result in Time Out.

Many parents think that they are using Time Out when they send a child to his room. But there are usually a couple of things wrong with this version of Time Out. For one thing, there are probably lots of things for Bobby to do in his room—read, play with toys, even watch TV. So getting sent to his room is not exactly like sending Shadrach, Meshach and Abednego to the fiery furnace. Another problem with sending a child to his room is that it causes him to associate his room with punishment, it becomes a place to be avoided, and a child's room ought to be a good place for him.

To get around these problems, the misbehaving child should be sent to an area that is not supposed to be a fun spot, a place that is dull and very unrewarding. A hallway, for example, or a chair in an untraveled room. The area you choose should be as barren as you can make it. No toys, people, radio, books, magazines, TV, preferably not even a window. The idea is to find a spot that is as dull as a piano recital. A place where the most exciting thing to do is count the spots on the ceiling.

Once you've selected a suitable area to use as a penalty box, you are ready to make use of Time Out. When the child misbehaves, place him in the penalty area. Explain to him that, since he can't behave properly in the living room, (the dining room, at the birthday party, etc.) he will have to spend some time in Time Out.

Once the child understands how Time Out works, you may only have to say to him, "Two minutes of Time Out."

Time Out should *always* be for a specified period of time and should always require *good behavior* to get out. For example, you might say, "I'll come and get you when you've been good for ten minutes," or "You can come out when you've been good for ten minutes." If a child gets off the chair he should not be rewarded for this behavior by being returned to the fun and games. If he is required to be well behaved for ten minutes, then his ten minutes begins all over again every time he leaves the chair. Ideally, the time out area should be out of earshot. If not, and he begins singing "99 Bottles of Beer on the Wall" at the top of his lungs or has a two minute tantrum, the ten minutes begins only after the curtain has fallen on his performance. This way, the *end* of Time Out is a reward for good behavior.

42

The first few times you use Time Out, Junior may try carrying on a ruckus. This is his way of retaliating: "Hah, this won't work," he may say. "I'll make so much noise they'll let me come out just to shut me up." If you do release him when he's noisy, it's all over: you may just as well hand him a dollar bill every time he does something obnoxious. If you ignore his tantrum in Time Out, you will be making use of the principle of extinction (chapter eight) and the behavior will disappear. When the tantrum starts, you may go to him *once* and remind him that he can't come out until he has behaved properly for ten minutes. Don't remind him any more than this or your attention may reinforce his misbehavior. It is also not necessary to add further penalties once a child is in Time Out. If he has tantrums, he is only punishing himself, since he will be in longer than necessary to get his release. Sooner or later he will realize that, and there is no need to add more penalties or punish him in other ways.

It is also not necessary to use long Time Out periods. Usually a few minutes is sufficient. After all, if after a ten minute penalty Junior comes back and misbehaves again, he goes right back to the penalty box. I suggest you try Time Out periods of five or ten minutes. If the conduct is particularly nasty, assign a fifteen minute penalty.

One advantage of Time Out is that it requires no emotion from the parent. Scolding a child often leads to the parent's getting upset and that can be rewarding to the child. If the child is able to make the parents angry, particularly to the point where they strike out at him, he is at that moment exercising an extremely high degree of control over them. He is controlling what they think, how they feel, what they are paying attention to, and even what they are doing. This represents almost complete control. Giving a little person this kind of control over a big person is overwhelmingly reinforcing. Thus, the reason why spankings often do not work is that *manipulating and controlling parents is far more important to the child than the pain of a spanking*. With Time Out you simply tell the child—once he knows how it works—"five minutes of Time Out, Billy." No shouts, no arguments. The parent is not the enemy, since Billy gets *himself* into Time Out and he gets himself out of it. The responsibility is his; the choice is his.

Time Out is best used when the child can be removed immediately from the situation that is providing the rewards for his misconduct. But sometimes a suitable penalty area is not available. If the family is at a theater, for example, you can't use Time Out without punishing yourself as well as Junior. Or if you're out for a Sunday drive you may not be able to use Time Out. And there are other times when Time Out may not be the best solution. Suppose, for example, that you find out Junior has disobeyed your rule that he must not drive the family car until he gets a license? What do you do then?

Well, what would a traffic court do if *you* were cited for driving without a license?

10

Fines

Time Out is a form of punishment that, like sending a criminal to prison, deprives him of reinforcers. But using Time Out makes sense only when some ongoing event is rewarding undesirable behavior. For example, if a child fails to do his homework or some household chore, Time Out just isn't appropriate. If Billy behaves rudely at his birthday party, you can sentence him to five minutes in Time Out. But what if the birthday party is at Molly's house, and you aren't there to apply Time Out? You will probably hear of the misdeed only after the party is over. In either of these situations, fines may be used very effectively.

A fine, like Time Out, is a form of punishment. It consists of taking away reinforcers. It rests on a principle very similar to the one that underlies the use of Time Out, namely that:

Behavior That is Followed by Removal of Reinforcers Tends to be Avoided

We usually think of a fine as an amount of money an offender has to pay. If the child is paid an allowance for various chores, he can be required to pay part of that in fines. But parents needn't restrict themselves to monetary fines. If you use tokens as rewards, then you can require payment of tokens as fines. Parents should think of a fine as a reinforcer that must be sacrificed by a child because of wrongdoing. He may have to "pay" with thirty minutes of TV time or an earlier curfew hour, or he might have to give up some privilege, such as the use of a bicycle or a car, for a specified period.

In one family a fourteen-year-old son was supposed to carry out the kitchen garbage daily. For years this simple chore had been the basis of endless hassles. His parents had resorted to constant nagging and threats to get the job done. "How can you do this to your mother? Wait 'til you have kids of your own: I hope they treat you the same way," his mother would complain. The father would join in with remarks like, "I hope you get run over by a garbage truck; that would be poetic justice."

It was then decided that the son would be reminded only once daily to take out the trash, and if it were not emptied by 8:00 p.m. the mother would perform this chore. Fifty cents would be deducted from the boy's allowance, however, and paid to the mother each time she had to carry out the garbage. The son was informed of these new rules, then nothing more was said to him.

On the third night, after he had not carried out the garbage for the first three days, he noticed his mother was doing so, but without nagging him. He inquired about the effect of this on his allowance and was told. The son then began to protest that the rule was unfair, but the parents refused to change their policy.

Allowance day came five days after the program was initiated, during which time the boy had not once carried out the garbage. He thus had two and a half dollars deducted from his three dollar allowance. When making payment, the mother dropped fifty cents into his hand in a rather prissy manner, which triggered another protest. The parents again listened, but without arguing, since that in itself might have been positively reinforcing; and they did not relent.

The next day the son carried out the garbage in the afternoon saying that he was not going to let the mother get his fifty cents and accusing her of tricking him into not carrying out the garbage so that she could get his money. From this point on, the garbage was never a problem.

Fines can also be used effectively with more difficult children, such as six-teen-year-old Gina. Note how one set of parents first mishandled a situation, then improved their management through the judicious use of fines:

Father: What's this your mother tells me about your not coming in until 1:30 in the morning? The very idea! In the old country, if I'd come in at 1:30 my father would have beaten me within a millimeter of my life.

Gina: (says nothing but allows father to rave on)

Father: What's all of this running around? What kinds of things are going on? It doesn't take until 1:30 in the morning to do decent things. Don't expect me to stand by and watch while you turn into some kind of a tramp.

Gina: (to herself) I'll sure be glad when I can get out of here.

Parental pontification, categorizing, labeling and evaluating with words like tramp, dampen Gina's spirits like a vaporizer. When her father makes her feel like some kind of walking venereal disease, it is understandable that she'd be anxious to leave home.

After receiving professional consultation, the parents first clearly stated a rule that the daughter would have to be in by 10:00 p.m. Sunday through Thursday, but could stay out until midnight on Friday and Saturday nights. She was told that she would lose the privilege of one night out for every fifteen minutes she was late on any night.

On the following Friday night the daughter came in forty-five minutes late from her date. The parents did not become upset or lecture her, but simply reminded her that she could not go out on Saturday, Sunday or Monday nights. Gina protested, stating she did not think the rules were fair and that she was required to come in too early. The parents agreed that any time she wanted to discuss the hours and could make a good case for coming in later they would be glad to consider a change. In the meantime, she would lose the privilege of going out the next three nights.

Gina came in late on very few occasions after that, and when she did, she readily accepted the consequences.

Notice that the penalty for coming in late on Friday had to be paid at the very first opportunity, that is, Saturday, Sunday, and Monday. (It is also important that parents not be dissuaded from collecting a fine however good a child's behavior may be between the violation and the time for paying the penalty.) Children will argue with parents, trying to convince them that their misbehavior was justified or simply trying to wear them down so that they will revoke the penalty. If you give in at these times, you will be rewarding the child not only for the original misconduct but for hassling you as well. Worst of all, you will be rewarding them on an occasional basis, making for more persistent behavior (see chapter six).

A common problem when there are two or more children in the family is sibling squabbling. Fines can be used effectively to put an end to this annoying behavior.

Young Douglas was continually coming up with something like, "Rhonda didn't feed the dog, so I get to take my bath last." On another day it was Rhonda who hollered, "Doug got some new clothes, so I get to sit by the window on our vacation."

Twelve-year-old Craig had a tendency to go beyond the usual limits of rivalry by hitting his seven-year-old sister, Carole. She, however, was known to have antagonized him on numerous occasions. His parents dealt with this by setting the rule that no child would be permitted to hit or bother another.

The victim was responsible for reporting any wrongdoing to the proper authorities (parents). Any child who hit another would be fined for doing this no matter how justified he thought the hitting may have been. Also, one child who was being bothered by another could report the offender and receive justice. The consequence was a quarter, payable to the sibling who had been bothered.

At first the children seemed to prefer taking the law into their own hands. They would retaliate rather than blow the whistle on the offender. The first instance of one turning in another came when Craig had been struck by his sister. He had apparently figured out that he could pester his sister, be hit by her without being hurt, and then turn her in. She would then have to cough up a quarter. This proved to be a significant learning experience for Carole, who began to turn Craig in for inappropriate behavior. After they got that out of their systems, the children became quite capable of asking their parents for help when they were being exploited by each other. Sibling rivalry soon decreased and the home atmosphere returned to a reasonable level of tranquility.

Sometimes the results of a child's misconduct persist long after the misdeed. If Mary fingerpaints a mural on the living room wall, her creative mischief will endure until someone cleans it up. That someone is usually Mom, though occasionally Dad may contribute a swish or two. In either case, the parent is unhappy because the child has added to the workday.

A fine will, of course, discourage the child from making a similar mess in the future, but the fine doesn't clean up the mess. In situations like this, parents often lose their tempers. They shout and threaten and sometimes they resort to physical violence. Oddly enough these practices don't help clean up the mess either.

Yet the parent, enraged, often misses the point, rages at the child, sometimes spanking him harshly—and then cleans up the mess. While doing so, he'll mumble things like, "I don't know what I did to deserve a child like that," or "I guess now I'm paying for my sins. Wow! High interest and inflation are everywhere." These parents are the ones you see flipping their lips with an index finger—the people who have shed so many tears they have varicose veins of the eyeballs. I would now like to introduce these parents to a really nifty invention.

The eraser.

11

Correction

The eraser is proof positive that Shakespeare was wrong when he said, ''What's done is done, and can n'er be undone.'' Psychologists—clever folks, those psychologists—have applied the eraser principle to children. No, I'm not referring to rubbing them out, or even to the long-sought ''morning-after pill,'' but to the fact that children are able to undo the damage they've done. If, for example, Mary is old enough to smear fingerpaint all over the wall, then she is old enough to wash fingerpaint off the wall. If Billy is adept enough to knock the garbage over, he is skilled enough to clean it up again. Psychologists have come up with a technical term for this procedure in which wrongdoing is corrected by the wrongdoer. They call it correction. Correction is based on the principle that:

When Behavior Produces Additional Work It Will Be Avoided

For example, if Ann has a habit of running into the house and slamming the door, she will learn to close the door properly if, after letting it fly, she is required to go back outside and come through the door slowly, closing the door gently. Sometimes children will resist this practice by taunting the parents—they will repeat the act but continue to slam the door, or they will close the door in exaggerated slow motion. This is intended to annoy the parent, and if it does, the result usually is that the parent will give up the technique. Then Ann can go back to her door slamming. But if Mom and Dad refrain from sarcasm and hostility, and simply, quietly require that the act be performed correctly, without getting emotional, without arguing with the child, then Ann should learn to close the door quietly—at least when Mom or Dad is around.

Of course, Ann's parents could levy a fine each time she slammed the door, and that might work just as well as making her correct her behavior. One disadvantage correction has is that it takes the time and attention of the parent. When Charles spreads the sheets over his bed and announces he has made it, you have to supervise the correction of his work. To many parents it would be easier to make the bed themselves, and of course, Charles will be hoping you will come to that conclusion. He may even prove to be remarkably slow at grasping the intricacies of bedmaking. You must remember, however, that the choice is not between making or not making his bed on this *one* occasion.

It may be that insisting that Charles correct his behavior will be time consuming and troublesome to you. If so, *over*-correction may be indicated. This is a way of upping the stakes so as to hasten the pace of learning. If Ann slams the door, she has to close it properly several times to make amends. If Charles messes up a bed, he gets to make two. With *over*-correction, he will soon learn it is less time consuming for himself to do the job properly in the first place. The advantage that correction has is that it clarifies what behavior is desired, whereas fines tell the child only what behavior is *not* desired. A fine tells the child what not to do, but doesn't spell out what the child *should* do. Correction leaves absolutely no doubt about what behavior is acceptable.

Another disadvantage to fines is that it guarantees that the child who is fined for not making his bed may feel that the fine is a price worth paying. In a sense, he pays his parent to be his maid! Seeing that the fine is not working, the parent may increase the penalty until it reaches so exorbitant an amount that the child will make the bed to avoid paying it. But by this time the parent has reached the uncomfortable position of being justly accused of levying unreasonable fines for a misdemeanor. With correction, there is a somewhat greater sense of justice, since the punishment tends to fit the crime.

Correction and over-correction are particularly good techniques to use when a child does his chores half-heartedly. Susan, for example, is in a hurry to get over to Janice's house for the slumber party. It is her job to do the dishes after dinner and, in her eagerness to leave the house, she does a poor job. Faced with this situation some parents will give a short lecture and then redo the dishes themselves. "Well," they will say, "I didn't want to make her late for the party." But if Susan is made to redo the dishes, who is it that has made Susan late? Isn't it Susan herself? Susan, we can safely predict, will disagree. "You'll make me late," she will undoubtedly protest. And Mr. and Mrs. Parent will be tempted to defend themselves, which will lead to an argument. Such arguments only weaken the effects of correction (or other punishment, such as fines or Time Out) since they are interpreted by the child as parental doubt. If you are sure you are right, what is there to argue about?

The parent who quietly insists that Susan redo the dishes will get results, and Susan will eventually realize that if she is late on such occasions it is her own fault, because instead of doing the dishes properly in fifteen minutes, she did them in twenty-five minutes—once improperly and once correctly.

Correction is an excellent way of getting rid of annoying or slovenly behavior. But there are some behaviors that can't be corrected. Billy can't erase the black eye he gives to Kenny. And while Time Out can be used to curb such tendencies, there are times when stronger measures are warranted.

This is where I make enemies of the Committee to End Violence Against the Next Generation.

12

To Spank Or Not To Spank

The old adage, "spare the rod and spoil the child," has gone by the boards. Corporal punishment seems to be frowned upon by psychologists, social workers, psychiatrists, teachers, and every other group of professionals who works with children. There are organizations, such as the Committee to End Violence Against the Next Generation, that vigorously oppose the use of physical punishment of any sort for any reason. Books are written about the rights of children and the evils of child abuse, as if every parent who ever spanked a child had no regard for the rights and dignity of children and was, in addition, a closet sadist.

Let me admit right off that it's a good thing that parents have become more cautious about using physical punishment and that there are such groups as the CEVANG that have made us sensitive to the fact that discipline can turn into brutality. I also want to make it clear that spanking has serious limitations as a way of modifying behavior. For one thing, if improperly administered, spankings can create a great deal of anxiety, and anxiety does not contribute to a healthy childhood. And the parent who spanks as a means of rejecting a child or expressing anger toward him runs the risk of isolating himself from the child: it's hard to feel close to someone who is frequently a source of physical and emotional pain. Another problem with spanking is that, as we saw in chapter seven, children acquire many of their habits by imitating their parents. One thing they may learn by being spanked is that physical force is an effective and acceptable way of dealing with other people. (Needless to say, this is seldom what the parent is *trying* to teach the child; nevertheless, it is often what he learns.)

Finally, spankings focus attention on what the child does wrong. Remember that one of the most common errors parents make is to ignore good behavior and respond to the child only when he misbehaves. Since attention is reinforcing, a child may learn to misbehave simply as a way of getting your attention—even though that attention takes the form of a spanking. (It's better than nothing.) It would be better for the parents to reward good behavior and ignore mischief than to ignore good behavior and punish mischief.

Despite all these limitations, I insist that, under certain circumstances, spanking is a responsible and appropriate action for a parent to take. Now, I realize that in some people's minds child psychologists who advocate spanking are tied with whooping cranes and the Himalayan ibex for Number One on the endangered species list, but at this point, I feel like saying, "trust me." At least stay with me for a while, long enough to give my ideas a chance. Then, of course, decide for yourself. For example, what do you do if a child behaves in a way that is dangerous to himself or to others? If your child likes to play in the middle of the railway tracks, you've got to do something that will produce quick results. And what if five-year-old Robert insists on picking up the baby and running around the house with him? Of course, you might try putting Robert on extinction (chapter eight) and simply ignore his moving-van game. Or you might use correction: every time Robert drops the baby, you could have him pick up and put down the baby properly. Trouble is, both of these tactics—and most others you might try—may take too long. They'll work, but by the time they do, you may have a slightly damaged baby on your hands. Therefore, as a matter of principle:

A Child Should Be Spanked When His Behavior May Be More Harmful To Himself Or Others Than The Spanking Itself

A smart slap on a child's bottom will do him a lot less harm than getting hit by a train. And while a spanking may hurt Robert, it will do much less damage than his baby sibling would receive from being dropped around the house like a spare toy; better that Robert have a bruised ego than that baby have a bruised brain.

There is absolutely no doubt that, properly applied, corporal punishment gets good results. But it must be administered according to certain rules. Suppose, for example, that four-year-old Virginia likes to play with Horace, the family pet. (Horace is a 200-pound boa constrictor.) Now, Horace is a sweet fellow, and ordinarily quite harmless. Ordinarily. But if teased, he has been known to become irritable, and an irritable 200-pound boa constrictor is no fit playmate for a four-year-old. Well, you've noticed that Virginia likes to bang on Horace's head:

"Hello Horace," pat, pat, pat, "Nice Horace," pat, pat, pat, "Oh, did I step on your tail Horace?" pat, pat, pat, "Come on out of your cage Horace. Let's play hide and seek," pat, pat, pat.

You can see that this could be dangerous. It might be a very good idea to get rid of Horace, or to store him in a place where Virginia can't get to him, but these solutions would mess up my example, so let's keep him around for a while longer. OK, then, since Horace stays and, presumably, you're not willing to sacrifice Virginia, you've got to figure some way of keeping her from becoming Horace's lunch. One thing to do is to explain and demonstrate the correct way to treat a boa constrictor. (Remember that punishment tells you only what you *shouldn't* do, not what you should do.) This should include a very simple statement about exactly what behavior is forbidden such as, "Don't touch the boa constrictor."

All right, you leave the room certain that Virginia knows what behavior is forbidden and what the consequences will be for breaking the rule. You return to the room and see her trying to give Horace a dental exam. What do you do?

1) The first thing to do is to say, "NO!" in a loud, clear voice. You don't need to scream, just be sure you get the child's attention. (Snakes are deaf, so you won't startle Horace.)

   Incidentally, many parents are inclined to give an additional warning, to remind the child of the rule. This is a mistake unless you really doubt that the child understood your instructions. Once the child understands the rules, the consequences should be swift and certain.

2) Next, slap the child smartly on the buttocks *once* with the flat of your hand. It is not necessary to make a big deal out of this. A formal "spanking ceremony" (throwing the child over your knee, etc.) is not helpful and unnecessarily humiliates the child. There is also no need to escalate the punishment by hitting the child several times; once should be enough. (If you insist on a more extensive spanking, chances are you're doing it to relieve your own tension, and that's not a good reason for hitting a child.) One reason that I encourage you to follow these limits on how you spank is that these restrictions will help you to keep from going into a rage. No matter how mischievous a child is, he should not have to see his Dad or Mom turn into a Mr. or Mrs. Hyde. Also, if there are bruises, cuts, or other injuries, you are either hitting the child too hard or there is something physically wrong with the child.

3) State the reason for the spanking in simple, concise language: "I spanked you because you were touching the boa constrictor." Period. End of lecture.

4) Introduce the child to some appropriate behavior. It is important to give the child the opportunity to be rewarded for good behavior. Punishment suppresses behavior, but it doesn't make the child forget the behavior. If you want to be sure that Virginia doesn't play dangerous games with Horace, be sure you reward her for playing safely with brother Vernon.

These are the steps to follow in using corporal punishment, but there are a couple of other things to keep in mind. As the examples above illustrate, you should punish misconduct *immediately*. It is always important to reward or punish a behavior as soon as the behavior occurs. If there is a delay of even a minute, some other behavior will occur and your reward or punishment may no longer have the desired effect. For example, what do you do when little Lori acts up at the supermarket? If you spank her in public, you get dirtier looks than a sheik at a Bar Mitzvah. The whole affair may turn out to be more of a punishment for the parent than the child. But if Lori's punishment is put off until Mother gets her home, the delay may render the punishment ineffective. What *can* be done is to pronounce the sentence immediately, although it might not be carried out until the child gets home. You might say, "For that, I will give you a spanking when we get home," or "The consequences for that will be one spank, but I'm not going to give it to you until we're in private." To some extent, the pronouncement of punishment is itself a punishment. This provides for imme-

53

diacy of consequences, but without having to make a scene. Rewards such as praise for behaving nicely should be given at the market *during* the good behavior.

One way that parents often delay punishment is to put the responsibility on the other parent. Traditionally, this takes the form of, "Just wait until your father comes home; then you'll get it." Not only will the spanking that Dad gives have little effect on misbehavior (since it comes long after the behavior), but Dad will find that he's an unwelcome guest in his own house.

Another point to remember is that if a child is to be spanked for some behavior, he should be spanked each time the behavior occurs, with no exceptions. Remember that each time the behavior occurs, it may be rewarding in some way; if you spank only occasionally, then the behavior is also rewarded occasionally. And you remember that occasional reinforcement is much more powerful in maintaining behavior than constant reinforcement. If the behavior is serious enough to warrant spanking, then the last thing you want to do is to let it be reinforced on an occasional basis. So, make no exceptions, give no pardons, offer no reprieves, make no compromises. If you are going to spank for a given misdeed, spank every time that misdeed occurs.

While my views on spanking may not be in vogue just now, I believe that the evidence is on my side. Not only that, I believe spanking can be far more desirable than other methods of punishment. A spanking, for example, may have less potential for making the child feel badly about himself than do other forms of "discipline and guidance" which are applied as alternatives. Let's look at some of the alternatives which many parents turn to in order to keep from spanking. They often involve lecturing to (or yelling at) the child. Not only can this be ineffective in decreasing a child's maladaptive behavior, but there is serious potential for lowering his self-concept. Other alternatives include loss of privilege, such as not being able to go out and play with friends. Such consequences, if over-used, can deprive the child of valuable social contacts which are important to his development, and no punishment that might hamper a child's development should ever be used. One nice thing about spankings is that they can be over and done with in a short period of time. They can also serve to remove any feelings of guilt that the child may harbor, since he is, in essence, paying for his wrongdoing. The absence of guilt is further aided if the spanking parent refuses to act as though the child is bad, but rather as though he had simply made an unwise decision (one which got him a spanking).

Another technique which parents rely on in lieu of spanking is generously referred to as "reasoning with the child." There is a widespread stereotype among laymen that the "good" parent is one who "reasons" with the child. I have observed that what most parents do in the name of reasoning seems both ineffective and degrading. They typically ridicule by saying such things as, "Why did you do that?" or "You know you shouldn't do that because ... " Reasoning is usually more a matter of badgering, criticizing, and verbally entrapping the child; it is often nothing more than an attempt to get the child to incriminate himself. Such tactics are usually ruled unfair in a courtroom, leaving open the question of how appropriate they are when used on a child in his own home.

54

One recent study has shown that parents who spanked were unlikely to withdraw love as a form of punishment. Those who didn't spank tended to rely heavily on rejection or withdrawal of affection. Given the choice, a spanking with love seems preferable to the absence of spanking accompanied by an absence of love.

The question of spanking may be a simple one for a parent of limited sophistication, but presents a more difficult choice for one who is well-informed. The sophisticated parent must consider the fact that great damage can be done if spankings are not administered appropriately. He knows that he does not have the right to hit his child, or to vent anger and rejection, simply because he is the parent. By the same token, he must consider that a spanking administered without hostility, which results from the child's breaking a clearly defined rule, may create fewer dangers than other alternatives. This concept of spanking administered with love was first brought to my attention by the book, *A Man Called Peter*, a biography by Catherine Marshall about her husband. He was a man of wisdom and compassion who for many years served as the chaplain of the United States Senate. Catherine Marshall described how, following a wrongdoing by their child, Peter Marshall and the son would go arm in arm into the library. In a few minutes they would emerge, still arm in arm, but the boy would have a tear in his eye. He had received a spanking, but showed neither a sense of guilt nor any feeling of resentment toward his father. The Marshall family's experience demonstrated that spankings can be carried out with love and dignity.

What I am advocating is spanking as an art form. An excerpt from a conversation between a skeptical parent and her twelve-year-old son may clarify the point:

Mother: I'm reading this paper by a psychologist who believes in spanking. What do you think about that?

Son: Are you going to start whipping me?

Mother: I don't know. I'm still trying to decide what I think about it.

Son: Spanking is really stupid!

Mother: Why do you say that!

Son: Because there are lots of other things that hurt so much more. (pause) That's the whole point, isn't it?

Mother: Yes, I think that is what he was trying to say.

Now if you have read this chapter carefully and if you apply spankings consistently and humanely in those occasional situations that call for spanking, if you are doing all this and the behavior persists, there is only one person to turn to. Uncle Remus.

13

Into The Briar Patch

Once upon a time, according to Uncle Remus, Brer Rabbit got into a real jam. He let himself get "cot up" by his arch enemy, the fiendish Brer Fox. After years of being outsmarted and made a fool of by the long-eared hare, Brer Fox wanted more than dinner: he wanted revenge. So Brer Fox set about to get even by trying to make Brer Rabbit sweat; the rabbit would suffer before he was transformed into a gourmet dish. But as Brer Fox built a fire and proceeded to boil a pot of water, telling his small meal how he would be transformed slowly, ever so slowly, into a rabbit stew, the crafty rabbit showed no sign of distress. Instead, he *thanked* Brer Fox for thinking up such a kindly way of bringing Brer Rabbit to his end. Brer Fox was astounded at the way Brer Rabbit chattered about the preparation of the meal. Brer Rabbit acted more like someone who was *coming* to dinner than someone who was going to *be* dinner. For Brer Fox, the equanimity of his long-eared meal was most disappointing. After all, foxes and rabbits were the cowboys and Indians of the animal world. It was unfair of Brer Rabbit to act as though he almost enjoyed the fiendish cruelty of his enemy. Brer Fox discarded the boiling water and announced that he would strip the hide off the rabbit and eat him alive.

"Oh," the rabbit said thoughtfully, "Rabbit sashime. Hmmm. Interestin' idea. Well, Brer Fox, you are being so kind-hearted about this. You know, I really did think you would do somethin' really mean to me, like throwing me in the briar patch."

Brer Rabbit began to sweat and squirm and sob. And Brer Fox began to grin. The more Brer Rabbit pleaded and squirmed, the wider Brer Fox grinned. Pretty soon Brer Rabbit looked like he ought to be fitted with a straight jacket, and Brer Fox was grinning from ear to ear. (I told you he was a fiend.) Brer Fox realized that the only end that frightened poor Brer Rabbit was being chucked into a thorny patch of briar bushes.

Never had Brer Fox seen such terror in any creature, but despite Brer Rabbit's loud protestations, he wound up and slung that rabbit into the middle of that briar patch. But instead of screaming and hollering, instead of being torn to shreds by the thousand barbs, Brer Rabbit sat contentedly among the thorns.

"Why, don't you know," the rabbit exclaimed, "that rabbits are born in briar patches? This is my *home*."

Now, what's the moral of this little story? If you say, "That rabbits like briar patches," you flunk. If you say, "There's no pleasing a rabbit," you're a bit closer. I'll give you a hint. Brer Fox thought that throwing Brer Rabbit into the briar patch would be very painful (a psychologist would say very aversive), something that Brer Rabbit wanted desperately to avoid. But Brer Rabbit's *behavior* showed that he did not find briar patches aversive. In fact, he found getting tossed into one very rewarding. Now, you and I both know that Brer Rabbit was dissembling when he claimed that he didn't mind the idea of getting boiled: things like that scared the hair off of him. But he behaved as though he practically liked being boiled, but hated the thought of being thrown into a briar patch.

The lesson is that the only way to tell whether something is reinforcing or punishing is by observing its effects. This is true of rabbits, children, and other small creatures who hop around a lot. I call this the Brer Rabbit principle:

Rewards and Punishments are Known By Their Effects

This is where life can get complicated for a parent, because everyone has his own unique hierarchy of rewards and punishments. In *1984,* Orwell's rebel hero finally broke down when threatened with the torture he feared most, being attacked by a rat. And I know a man who weighs over 200 pounds who panics whenever butterflies or moths come near him. Then, on the other hand, there are people who will do practically anything for certain foods; the alcoholic, for example, is a person who finds alcohol inordinately reinforcing. Heroin addicts are the same way about their drug. Obese people obviously find food very reinforcing, while skinny people may take it or leave it. The point is that people differ, and what is terribly rewarding to one person may be terribly punishing to another: You like chocolate ice cream? It makes me sick. You're afraid of water? I love it.

Children, like people, differ. One child's cooperative behavior may increase rapidly when rewarded with praise from a parent, while the same praise may have no effect on the cooperative play of another child. A child who likes to bully his smaller siblings may not respond to Time Out treatment, but a fine of one token may change his behavior in a hurry.

To make matters worse, children change. One day, nothing in the world is so rewarding to Eddie as going for a ride in the family car with Mom and Dad. He will work like the devil to earn the right to go for a ten-minute ride. Next day he couldn't care less.

Of course, most parents have a pretty good idea about what their child finds rewarding and punishing. But they don't always keep in mind that the power of a reward or a punishment is determined by the results it produces.

One way to keep tabs on what a child finds reinforcing is to notice how he spends his time when left to himself. Does he watch TV? If so, watching TV will be reinforcing. Does he ride his bike? Build model planes? Make soap carvings? Read? If he does, then these activities can probably be used to reward good behavior. Or tokens can be keyed to these activities so that the child can buy a model plane, soap carving, books, etc. Some parents can come up with nothing better than corny rewards like the famous gold-star-on-the-wall-chart. The uncommitted parent sometimes chooses ineffective reinforcers, and then throws up his hands, labeling the child a special case or denying the validity of reinforcement principles. What is needed instead is more sensitivity to whether reinforcers are working, and what new ones might be tried if initial attempts fail. The best approach is not to think of children in general, but to make careful observations of *your* child. Such observations should determine what works with him. When reinforcements are hand picked according to a given child's preferences, change should result quickly.

It is also essential to remember that every child has his own little individual reinforcement hierarchy. The number one reinforcement for one child may be number 431 for another. Most parents make their mistake in stereotyping rewards. Actually, there is no such thing as a universal secondary reinforcement, that is, something which is rewarding for everyone. It depends on the child. Some parents complain: "My child doesn't respond to rewards. I've given him money, and I could praise him a million times and it wouldn't do any good." Or, "I told her if she'd make all C's or higher on her grade card during her junior year, I'd buy her a new car, but she just didn't seem interested." Parents who are not getting any mileage out of their use of rewards often feel that the principles of reinforcement don't work. But, there is nothing wrong with these principles; rather, the particular rewards and punishments are simply not the best-suited for that particular child. If a child does something repeatedly, it is bound to be paying off in some way. For instance, we often provide rewards when we think we are punishing, and vice versa. A classic illustration of this involves the classroom teacher who finally becomes fed up with Jonathan and screams at him. The teacher may think she is punishing "rule-breaking behavior," when in fact she is probably rewarding "attention-getting behavior." Or, when grandmother comes for a visit and greets the children with a kiss, nine-year-old Mary finds these expressions quite desirable and therefore rewarding. But Greg, who is eleven, feels uncomfortable. Thus, the same response from Grandmother can be a reward for one child and a punishment for the other.

Another subtlety of the reward/punishment rule is that we often think that one form of behavior is being dealt with when, in fact, it is another. Most parents move with lightning speed if they see their child probing about a light socket with a hairpin. Yet this situation may be oversimplified as far as the kinds of behavior that are at stake. Only part of this act involves dangerous ("getting yourself killed") behavior. Another part reflects the child's tendency to explore. Realizing this, parents will need to consider not only ways of diverting the child away from dangerous acts, but how to do so without stifling his need to explore.

I can relate a personal experience when two kinds of behavior became entangled in a single act. For years, our family has enjoyed Longhorn cheese, and many times when the children were in grade school it was served on our plates before mealtime. Biting into the round cheeses altered their shape, and sometimes in the children's minds, the cheeses were transformed into dinosaurs. The kids picked them up and played with them as though they were toys. On occasions, fights even broke out between two cheeses. "My cheese can whip your cheese!" would become a challenge, betraying a smidgen of sibling rivalry. As middle-class parents, my wife and I had a "hand-on-a-hot-stove" reflex to correct the children about their manners, until careful consideration allowed us to realize that, in addition to bad manners, there was a certain amount of creativity involved in this activity. After all, the child who can look at a piece of cheese and see a prehistoric animal may possess the type of creativity that will some day make him president of General Motors. The challenge to us as parents then became to encourage socially acceptable table manners while not squelching creativity.

So, a reason why Brer Rabbit's Law is so important is that rewards and punishments can become a briar patch in which the parent gets ensnared. Parents may actually reward behavior they are trying to punish, or punish behavior they think they are rewarding. For example, a psychologist wanted to see what effect reprimands would have on the behavior of children. He asked their first grade teachers to announce to the children that they were no longer permitted to put pens, pencils or crayons into their mouths or touch their mouths in other ways. The teachers were also asked to reprimand a child whenever they saw him violating the new rule. Obviously, most people would consider getting reprimanded by a teacher a form of punishment; certainly most teachers think of it this way. But what the psychologist found was that the reprimands increased the unwanted behavior. Reprimands were rewarding.

Now, this classroom example may not hold in your family. But there is no doubt that parents can reward behavior they *think* they are punishing or punish behavior they *think* they are rewarding. The only way to tell is by looking at the results. If you think you are punishing some unwanted behavior, but it persists or even increases, then you may somehow be rewarding it unintentionally. Or if you think you have withdrawn the rewards that maintain a behavior, but it persists, perhaps there are other reinforcers you have neglected. If you don't get the results you expect, you can be very sure you are breaking Brer Rabbit's Law.

And if you aren't, someone else is. To find the culprit, you may have to look here, there and everywhere.

14

Here, There And Everywhere

Miss Smoot was a good old gal. She taught elementary school for two or three centuries, at least, and she knew what was what. It wasn't that she was mean; she terrified no one. The tiny soft-spoken lady looked as though a cross word would kill her, but when the kids went into her class, they behaved like little angels. Whenever the school principal wanted to show off the school to visitors, he'd bring them to Miss Smoot's class.

"And this class was recently released on parole from the State Training School," he'd say, inviting his guests to poke their heads through the back door of the room. What he didn't show them was how those children behaved in Mr. Hilding's class. Mr. Hilding was six feet tall, weighed 240 pounds (approximately 150 pounds more than Miss Smoot) and looked like Boris Karloff. In his class the kids were terrified—the first day. After that, they terrified him. Mr. Hilding just couldn't seem to keep control. It wasn't that he was too gentle. He shouted far more than Miss Smoot ever did, or could, and when he lost his temper (which was about once every ten minutes) he'd grab some little devil by the shoulders and shake him until his teeth came loose.

Now, I know that you knew a Miss Smoot, though she probably had a different name, and you probably knew a Mr. Hilding. The kids in your class would be little angels with Miss Smoot and then they'd go down the hall and raise hell in Mr. Hilding's room. It was as though there was some sort of magic vapor in the respective rooms that changed the children's personalities.

If you're like most people, you've probably always thought of the difference between Miss Smoot and Mr. Hilding as a difference in their personalities. Mr. Hilding, the kids would say, doesn't know how to handle a class. Miss Smoot is nice, so all the kids behave well. Mr. Hilding is too easy, and so on. Now, I hope you will look on Miss Smoot and Mr. Hilding and focus on what they *did*, not what they *were*; if you do, I think you'll see that they behaved very differently. Miss Smoot applied the principles we've discussed in previous chapters while Mr. Hilding didn't.

What I want you to notice, though, is that while Miss Smoot may have applied the principles of behavior beautifully, rewarding good behavior, extinguishing bad behavior, it did not have much effect upon what the kids did outside of her class. They were angels in her class but once they left the confines of those four walls, their angelic wings dropped to the floor and their ears took on a pointed look.

How come? If focusing on behavior and applying the principles of reward and punishment are so powerful, why didn't their good effects carry over into Mr. Hilding's class? And more importantly, if your efforts at emulating Miss Smoot are only going to improve your child's behavior in your presence—with the dear child turning into a monster at school, with the baby sitter, at summer camp, etc., etc.—then, what's the use of all your fine efforts? You can't follow him around the rest of his life rewarding and punishing behaviors.

What we're talking about here is what psychologists call *response generalization*. Once behavior has been established in one situation, it may occur in other situations. Unfortunately, most behaviors do not generalize from one situation to another, which is why Miss Smoot's good work did not carry over into Mr. Hilding's class. For the parent, the question of how to increase response generalization is very important.

It will help to know this principle:

Behavior Varies Over Time and Across Situations As The Reinforcers For Behavior Vary

What this means to the parent is that consistency is all-important.

If Dewey behaves uncooperatively, you know that you must reward him for cooperative behavior. Reward cooperative behavior today, tomorrow and the next day. And the day after that. Reward cooperative behavior in the living room, in the bedroom, in the kitchen, while driving down the road, while playing in the yard.

If you work on increasing cooperative behavior only when Dewey plays in the living room, you will get more cooperative behavior there—but you might not get much more cooperation when Dewey is in the basement or when he's playing in the yard. You will, in effect, be setting up a Miss Smoot environment in the living room, and a Mr. Hilding environment everywhere else. So be consistent: reward desirable behavior in as many situations as you can; withhold rewards for undesirable behaviors in as many situations as you can. And if behavior is to be punished, it should be punished in as many situations as possible. Be consistent over time and across situations.

The goal of consistency will be a lot easier to achieve if you can enlist the help of other people. You cannot call a meeting of the world and insist that everyone reward Dewey's cooperative acts and ignore his uncooperative behavior. But you can talk with your spouse about what behaviors you are trying to increase and work out an agreement concerning rewards and punishments. And your efforts will be a lot more successful if both parents offer the same number of tokens for a response and if both agree that the punishment for eating paint chips is one slap.

You can also explain to other members of the family, teachers, babysitters, etc., what you are doing and ask for their help. In fact, you may be surprised to find that if you reward them for going along with your plans ("Hey Sally, you rewarded Dewey nicely for that behavior") that their helpfulness will increase.

If there is an in-law or other adult who refuses to go along with you, you must either convince him to stay out of it or somehow remove the child from his influence. For example, if three-year-old Melinda has temper tantrums every time she is forbidden to do something, you will probably put her on extinction. Despite the racket, you ignore her, you say nothing to her, neither comfort nor scold her, and you refrain from picking her up. It begins to pay off, and then along comes Grandma who can't stand to see her precious darling cry. She picks up Melinda, comforts her and offers to buy her a castle in Scotland if it'll make her happy. Melinda, of course, stops crying and Grandma turns to you and says, "See, you just have to understand kids." What Grandma doesn't understand, though, is that she's just reinforced tantrums!

Clearly, you will get nowhere trying to extinguish tantrum behavior with Grandma around. Once she leaves, you may begin to make progress, but each time Grandma comes back, it will be a signal to little Melinda to turn on the screams. Grandma will give her what she wants. Again we have Miss Smoot and Mr. Hilding.

The only solution that I know of to a problem of this sort is to get Grandma to cooperate or keep her away. Then, next time Grandma rewards a tantrum, you just quietly say, "I'll get your hat and coat" (hopefully she hasn't just driven 800 miles). If you think this action too harsh, then instead of removing Grandma, you might remove Melinda. At the first signs of a tantrum in Grandma's presence, you escort Melinda to an area out of Grandma's reach. Do this quickly and without comment (you don't want to reinforce the tantrums yourself) and put Melinda in a bedroom. Lock the door if necessary to keep Grandma out. And *don't* argue with Grandma unless you want to reinforce *her* for interfering.

If there are other children in the family, you may be able to get their help. You don't necessarily need to explain the principles behind your behavior, just state what action is to be taken:

Mom: (to eight-year-old Ron) You know that Melinda has temper tantrums. When she does this I want you to ignore her *completely*. Don't even talk to her when she carries on. Just leave the room: then when she is quiet again, you can come and play with her.

Ron: But she'll cry for hours!

Mom: I realize that it will be unpleasant for all of us, but eventually she will learn that crying won't get her anywhere. Then she'll quit.

Other people who come into contact with your child can also be brought into the act. If Melinda has learned she can get what she wants by having tantrums , I guarantee you that she will persist in that behavior anywhere and anytime it will be rewarded: if it isn't rewarded at home, then she won't do it there; but if her nursery school teacher continues to reward tantrums, there will be tantrums galore at nursery school. And if the babysitter isn't brought in on the plan, there will be tantrums at home when the parents are out. Children learn that what doesn't pay off in one place at one time may pay off in another place at another time. (Kids are not as dumb as they look.)

Consistency from situation to situation and from individual to individual is important when you want to increase a desirable behavior, too. Allen, for example, is a poor reader. Nothing will get a student further behind in school than being a poor reader. Allen's mom and dad decide to reinforce reading in hopes that the more time Allen spends reading the more his reading will improve. When Allen finishes a book, they take him on a special trip to the library or a bookstore. They let him pick out books for himself (at his age level). They praise him when they see him reading, they listen to him talk about what he has read, and they read to him and let him read to them. All of which delights Allen, so his interest in reading increases steadily. Allen's parents bring their baby-sitter in on the plan along with the grandparents. When Allen misbehaves, he is not told ''Go sit in the corner and read a book!'' This turns reading into punishment. And when grandparents visit, they make a point of asking Allen about the books he has read, and as a special treat, they might give him a book as a reward for good behavior. All of this makes reading a fun thing, something to look forward to rather than avoid. And if Allen is rewarded in a variety of situations by a number of people, this consistency will produce remarkably good results in a relatively short time.

Consistency means that if a behavior is to be rewarded, it is rewarded by as many people and in as many situations as possible. Consistency does not necessarily mean, however, that every response is reinforced. Remember that in chapter six I pointed out that, once a behavior is well-established, it can be maintained with occasional reinforcement.

If Lynn is now cooperating regularly instead of squabbling, then it would be a good idea for the parents to discontinue rewarding *every* cooperative response. They might decide to reward about one out of every two cooperative efforts. Then they might raise the ante to approximately three cooperative responses, and so on. Fine. Consistency requires only that everyone who is involved in rewarding Lynn be in on the revised plan.

If extinction or punishment is being used to decrease a behavior, then consistency requires that everyone involved either withhold all rewards or punish in the same way for the same response. If Lynn is to be punished for combativeness, then everyone must understand what is considered a punishable response. It is not a good idea to have Mom punishing Lynn when she merely raises a threatening fist, while Dad punishes only if Lynn jumps on someone's face with both feet.

Consistency also requires that the punishment be the same regardless of who it comes from or where it occurs. If combativeness is defined as any potentially painful physical contact (a blow, a shove, a kick, etc.) and the punishment is a fine of five tokens, that behavior (painful physical contact) should *always* result in Lynn's being fined five tokens, regardless of where her aggressiveness occurs or who is around.

It is impossible to achieve one hundred percent consistency. There will be times when you will not be able to reward or punish a response even though you know you should. There will be other times when you will not be around and you may not be able to get the cooperation of the adult in charge. A teacher, for example, may resent your telling him how to do "his job." But the closer you come to perfect consistency, the better the results will be.

The next step is easy, as long as you aren't afraid of being bitten.

15

Get Close, They Won't Bite

There's an old saying, "close only counts in horseshoes and hand grenades." But within a family closeness counts a great deal. The more you are intimate, the more likely children are to imitate. This is only one reason why it's important to develop a relationship with your children. Another is that rearing children is a lot more fun if parents and children share a bond. But the most important reason for getting close to your children is the principle that:

Intimacy Is Essential To The Healthy Development Of Every Child

Intimacy implies physical contact, but it means much more than hugs and kisses. Sometimes people feel very close to each other but rarely hug or kiss; and some people hug and kiss each other all day long without true intimacy. And intimacy is not another word for love. Many parents love their children dearly, but are not intimate with them. The best synonym for the kind of intimacy I'm talking about is safety. When you feel secure with another person, you feel free to be yourself, you don't feel that you have to be on your guard, to pretend that you're something you aren't. Hugs and kisses are all over the place, but true intimacy, as I've defined it here, is as rare as an honest used-camel salesman.

A child who does not experience intimacy, particularly in early childhood, will have problems. For one thing, most psychotherapists believe that a child who does not form a close, secure relationship with at least one adult will have difficulty establishing intimate relationships in adulthood. They may have trouble dating, forming close friendships, getting along with a spouse. And it will also be very difficult for them to form intimate relationships with their own children. Children who do not feel close to an adult also often grow up with important personal hang-ups. Though they may, in fact, be loved dearly, without intimacy they may not feel loved. This results in very low self-esteem (see chapter eighteen). Sometimes these people develop what psychologists call an existential neurosis: they feel apart from other people and that somehow they don't fit in; they lack clear goals and values; and they have no sense of identity of who they are.

So intimacy is important. It may also seem to be the most natural thing in the world, and for some parents it is. But a great many parents (particularly those who were not close to their parents) do not know how to go about getting close to their children. Where does such a parent begin? How does he get close to his children?

Begin with behavior. (Remember chapter two?) There are three characteristics that one often sees in people who are close to each other, who feel safe with each other. First, they have a lot of eye contact: they look each other in the eye more often than strangers or casual acquaintances do. Second, they touch each other more than they touch other people. Touching does not necessarily mean hugging and kissing; it may mean simply putting a hand on a person's shoulder for an instant. Third, they talk to each other. This doesn't mean that one lectures the other, or that they engage in superficial chatter. It means they share true (hopefully deep) thoughts and feelings.

So if you want to have a closer, more intimate relationship with your child, you should begin to adopt these three characteristics. That is, you should make eye contact more often, touch more, have more conversations in which both parties share their deepest concerns.

I'm not suggesting that you stare at the kid like a cobra watching a plump mouse, or that you schedule bear hugs every ten minutes on the hour or that you use the child inappropriately as your confessor. But begin to adopt this behavior.

At first, these changes may seem artificial, and you may feel uncomfortable. (If it feels really weird, you're probably trying to change too quickly.) Eventually, you'll find that what used to feel strange begins to feel quite natural.

You may doubt that better eye contact, increased touching or even more intimate conversations will establish the *feeling* of intimacy. But give it a try. I think you'll find that as your behavior changes your feelings change too. Your child will also respond: as you become more intimate, he will begin to feel safer and will respond in a more intimate fashion. He'll also imitate your behavior.

This process may take time. If you've always been rather aloof with your sixteen-year-old son, and then all of a sudden you start putting your arm around him, *he's* going to feel uncomfortable even if you don't. So the older your children are, the more gradually you must change your behavior. But the potential gains of establishing a close relationship with your children will be worth the time and effort.

Increasing eye contact and increasing physical contact are both pretty much self-explanatory, and as long as you increase these behaviors gradually, you should have no problem with them. But the third change I've suggested, talking with the child, is another matter. With the popularity of television, conversation is pretty much a lost art, both between adults and between parents and their children. Parents do a great deal to undermine intimacy when they discourage their children from talking with them.

When Greg approaches his parents about a topic, they do everything but surgically close his mouth. Of course parents always have good reasons for their behavior. Sometimes they're too busy:

Greg: Mom, the house is on fire.

Mom: Not now, Greg I'm reading the paper.

Or too tired:

Greg: (holding his arm which seems to have two extra elbows) Dad, I just fell down the cellar steps.

Dad: (lying on the sofa, his head covered by a newspaper) Uh-huh.

Greg: I think I broke my arm.

Dad: That's nice.

Greg: But the bone is sticking out.

Dad: Uh-huh.

Greg: But don't you think we should go to the hospital?

Dad: Oh, Greg, you're always coming up with excuses to go somewhere. Can't you see I'm tired?

Or what the child has to say just doesn't interest the parent:

Greg: Mom, I got an A on my history test. It was all about George Washington.

Mom: That's nice. Why don't you tell you Dad about it?

Greg: He said I should tell you.

Mom: Well, tell me about it later.

Oddly enough, these parents will later complain that their child is remote, that they can't reach him. The child acts as though he's too busy to talk with his parents:

Mom: Greg, why didn't you *tell* me the rain was pouring in through the ceiling?

Greg: Well, I was in the middle of fixing my model airplane.

Or as though he's tuckered out:

Mom: Greg, your teacher called again. He says you're getting F's in all of your subjects. How do you think you'll graduate? I mean, here you are in the fifth grade flunking all your subjects.

Greg: Yeah, yeah, let's talk about it later. I want to take a nap now.

Mom: But if we don't straighten this out, you'll flunk fifth grade again.

Greg: So I'll be a little older when I graduate. Big deal.

Mom: But, Greg, you're already twenty-two!

Or as though talking with his parents is a bore:

Dad: Greg, I think I'm having another heart seizure.

Greg: (watching TV) Yeah, in a minute.

Dad: Not in a minute! Didn't you hear what I said, (gasp) I'm having (gasp, wheeze) a heart attack.

Greg: OK, OK, I heard you already.

Dad: Greg, (gasp, gasp) for God's sake (Wheeze, wheeze) get . . . . the medicine . . . . ..

Greg: Could you hold it down a little Dad, I can't hear what the Indian and the Masked Man are saying.

OK, I'm exaggerating. A little. But the point is valid: When parents fail to encourage their kids to talk with them, intimacy fails. Then we wonder why

69

there's a generation gap. Although talking about any subject is good, we miss a special opportunity if we neglect the opportunity to discuss deeper topics, say for example, fear. There's an old saying, "You can't make a silk purse out of a sow's ear." But the manufacturing of intimacy from an encounter with a frightened child may be an exception.

Mr. Carpenter was a hardworking, successful rancher in his late forties. He married somewhat late in life, and his only child was ten-year-old Dwight. The episode in question happened one night when he had finally fallen exhausted into bed after midnight. "I felt I'd been ridden hard and put up wet," he recounted. Dwight came into his room and the conversation went like this:

Dwight: I can't go to sleep.
Father: What in the world are you doing up at this hour?
Dwight: I can't sleep.
Father: Try harder.
Dwight: (makes no comment)
Father: Come on, I'm taking you back to bed.
Dwight: (complies, and says nothing)
Father: Here, I'll tuck you in.
Dwight: Okay.
Father: Are you afraid of something?
Dwight: Yes.
Father: What on earth is it?
Dwight: The Blob and the Fly.
Father: Those characters in the science fiction movie you saw on TV?
Dwight: Yeah.
Father: That's ridiculous, now you go to sleep.

Some parents might have been more sympathetic and allowed Dwight to remain in their bedroom. That however, would not foster intimacy so much as it would dependency or manipulation. The following illustrates how the situation might have been better used as a means of promoting intimacy:

Dwight: I can't sleep.
Father: I'm sorry. Would you like for me to take you back to bed and tuck you in?
Dwight: Yeah.
Father: You seem frightened.
Dwight: Yeah.
Father: Do you want to tell me about it?
Dwight: It's the Blob and the Fly.
Father: You're afraid they're going to get you?
Dwight: Yeah.
Father: I know how bad it is to be afraid. I was afraid a lot myself when I was your age. I used to hear noises, and I didn't know what they were. I imagined all kinds of things, and it scared the fire out of me.
Dwight: Really?
Father: Yes, and of course I'm still scared of things today.
Dwight: Oh, no, you're not.

Father: Yes, I am. Just the other night there were some lights over on the north end of the place. I thought it was rustlers, so I went to see. It turned out to be a bunch of kids having a weiner roast, nothing to be afraid of.

Dwight: I bet you were glad.

Father: (tucking the boy in bed and noting fewer nonverbal signs of anxiety) Yes, I was glad. You seem to be feeling a little better now. Do you think you can go to sleep?

Dwight: Well, I don't think I'm afraid of the Fly anymore, but I'm still afraid of the Blob. You can't kill it. They just took it up to the North Pole and froze it.

Father: (smiling understandingly) You're not sure it won't thaw out, right?

Dwight: Right!

Father: Goodnight. I love you.

Dwight: I love you, too.

Another mistake that parents make is to think that having a talk with a child means giving a lecture. Some parents' description of themselves is more uplifting than a Maidenform bra. It's nothing short of a miracle that some of us ever reached adulthood, considering how we had to trudge through blizzards to get to school, work from sunup to sundown, and go for days without enough to eat.

Father: Craig, bring in the milk from the front porch.

Craig: (bringing in the milk) Wow, it's cold out there!

Father: Cold? It's 15 degrees above zero. Let me tell you about cold. When I was your age, I lived on a farm. Sometimes the snow was so deep we had to jump up to spit. We had to walk to school in the cold—we didn't have any buses to take us there in luxury—sometimes the temperature was 40 below zero. You kids have got it too soft.*

The kid makes a comment about the weather and gets a lecture on the degeneration of the human species. That's going to foster intimacy? We have a much better shot at getting close to our children if we admit that we're only human than if we try to make the child think there's an "S" on our tee shirt and we change clothes in a phone booth. When a parent is willing to admit that he falls slightly short of perfection, a conversation might go like this:

Bruce: (age sixteen) Will you buy me a new jacket to sew my football letter on?

Father: Yes, your Mom and I talked about it and decided we could spring for a new jacket.

Bruce: Can we go get it now?

Father: We'll go tomorrow after I get home from work. You're proud of that letter aren't you?

Bruce: Sorta.

Father: We're proud of it too. You know you've been able to do something I was never able to do.

Bruce: What's that?

---

*February 31, 1950 in Alamosa, Colorado, the temperature was actually 40 below zero and some kids actually did walk to school.

Father: Earn a letter in football.

Bruce: Really? You mean you never earned one?

Father: No, I tried, but I never made it.

The fact that Bruce's father presents himself as human can only increase the chance that Bruce will feel closer to his father and be willing to share his fears and weaknesses.

Any parent who is overly critical also runs the risk of destroying intimacy, since the child will sense that anything disclosed may be used against him. For those of us who married long ago and are well on our way to resembling atrophied toads, our hairiness, bustiness, musculature and freedom from pimples may no longer be what makes or breaks us. Adolescents, on the other hand, can be more sensitive about their physical traits than asthmatics at a ragweed festival. Even the mildly negative reactions of parents can engender strong feelings of self-depreciation; that, in turn, works against our attempts to establish an intimate relationship. Parents are sometimes unintentionally critical:

Jenny: (age twelve, preparing to put on her first pair of hose)

Father: What do you think you're doing?

Jenny: What does it look like I'm doing? I'm putting on these hose.

Father: The heck you say; you aren't really going to do that are you?

Jenny: Yes, why not?

Father: Well, your legs are too skinny; with skinny legs like yours, hose would make you look just terrible.

Jenny: (leaving room in tears) I hate you.

Father: Don't get smart or I'll give you what's coming to you.

Jenny: (later on, talking with her mother) Mom, Daddy said my legs were too skinny to wear hose.

Mother: Your legs are thin, but thin legs can be very beautiful and stylish; most models are thin.

Jenny: I'd still give anything if I weren't so thin.

Mother: Has that been worrying you?

Jenny: Yes, I think I am the skinniest girl in my class.

Mother: That must bother you a lot.

Jenny: Well, it was bothering me, but after talking to you, it doesn't seem as bad now.

Father's behavior, of course, generated about as much intimacy as a kick in the shins. On the other hand, mother's uncritical approach and her genuine interest and warmth are ideally suited to fostering a close relationship.

Some parents complain they can't get close, especially to their teenagers, because they never see them. "We never see our son," complained one father. "He either stays away from home altogether or hides in his room. He never eats with us. It's like we're not the parents of a real boy. He's just a shadowy figure at the refrigerator door or a voice that mutters 'Aw, c'mon Sandra' over the phone in his room at thirty-minute stretches." All this means is that establishing closeness may require you to find some mutual interest (anything from sports to frogs) to talk about. It may involve some game (be it Old Maid or arm wrestling) which you can play with him.

One of my own children was like a bear; he expressed his affection by swatting people. I have awarded a "Purple Heart for Parents" medal to my wife for determination and bravery in meeting the challenge of closeness. Her attempts to hug and kiss him were as welcome as splinters, and she eventually realized that pushing, shoving and otherwise roughhousing was the way in which this child interacted with those to whom he was closest. So, she decided to engage in a little friendly pushing and shoving to promote physical contact. One evening our little gladiator, following the good-natured leads of his mother, stood in the doorway blocking her exit from a hall. She tried in fun to push him aside, and a friendly jostling match ensued. Suddenly, Brooks made a tackle, dropping Mom like a bad habit. A blood vessel in her leg was ruptured and she wound up on crutches for three weeks. This "clout" had a silver lining, however. Mom handled the accident in a way that prevented the son from developing feelings of guilt, and his expressions of concern for her resulted in a deeper intimacy.

There are other principles that will help you to get close to your child. In the next chapter, for example, I'll explain why, if you really want to know something, you won't ask.

16

Questions Are Not The Answer

"Why is it," a patient once asked his psychiatrist, "that you always answer a question with a question?" To which the psychiatrist replied, "How long has this been bothering you?"

Questions bother a lot of us. In fact:

Asking Questions Inhibits Communication And Diminishes Intimacy

Not all questions are bad, of course. If somebody asks if you've seen the magazine section of the Sunday paper, you're not likely to get upset. But a lot of questions convey more than a request for information, and unfortunately, these are the kinds of questions that a lot of parents like to ask most. Notice how familiar the following sounds:

Ida: Mom, Dale keeps calling me on the phone and talking for a long time. I'm not sure whether I like him or not.

Mother: How much have you talked to him? Has there been enough communication between the two of you for you to know whether or not you like him?

Ida: Well, I haven't talked to him very many times.

Mother: How do you know if you really like a boy?

Ida: Well, I guess I go by how I feel inside.

Mother: Do you think that's a very good standard? Sometimes people who are not the right kind can make you like them, but good people may not be too appealing at first.

In this example, Mom's questions are actually disrupting rather than facilitating communication. Ida wants to get some things off her chest, to sort of explore them a bit. But Mother's questions put Ida on the defensive; Mother isn't interested in having a conversation, in exchanging information or views, she's interested in manipulating her daughter to do what she (Mother) thinks is best. She is certainly not creating the kind of security that Ida needs to feel close to her mother.

And in the next example, Dad is so good at asking questions that he muffs a really good chance to get closer to his daughter:

Nancy: (age eight, and in the hospital to prepare for an appendectomy the following day) Dad, I've decided I don't want to have the operation.

Father: What's bothering you about it?

Nancy: I don't think I really need it. I feel pretty good now.

Father: What do you think would happen to you if you left the hospital without the operation and then had a sudden attack?

Nancy: What?

Father: You'd die.

Nancy: But people die in the hospital too. You remember three years ago, my friend Mary Anne died in the hospital.

Father: What are you worried about?

Nancy: The doctors, the hospital, the operation, the whole thing!

Father: Do you know what percentage of the people who have operations die as a result of reactions to anesthetic?

Nancy: No.

Father: Not very many, probably less than one percent.

Nancy: I don't care.

Father: Have you thought of anything you can do to get this off your mind or to make yourself feel better?

Nancy: No, I just think about it all the time.

Father: Do you think that's a good approach? Don't you think you can do better than that?

Nancy: I don't know.

Father: Well, you've got to have the operation, so you might as well accept it.

Nancy: (sobs quietly)

Another problem with questions is that they accuse. Think for a moment, about who asks questions: school teachers (Did you do your homework?), bosses (Why are you late?), lawyers (Where were you on the night of June 22nd?), and IRS auditors (You want to claim *how* much??????). These questions imply criticism, they accuse.

The parent who tries to strain or force an adolescent into intimacy through excessive probing will probably wind up with an emotional hernia. As an example, look at the effect of questions in the following example:

Mother: Where have you been?

Elaine: To church.

Mother: Well it's almost 10:30 and church was over at 8:30. Where did you go after church?

Elaine: To a fellowship. It's a party-like thing they have after church.

Mother: Who did you go with?

Elaine: Well, I walked over there from church with Roger Smith, but I really wasn't *with* anybody; we just walked together.

Mother: What did you do at the party?

Elaine:	Oh, we just sat around and talked and played games.
Mother:	What kind of games did you play?
Elaine:	Charades and stuff like that.
Mother:	How did you get home?
Elaine:	Roger walked me home.
Mother:	What did you two do when you were walking home?
Elaine:	Nothing. We just talked.
Mother:	Did he hold your hand?
Elaine:	Sometimes.
Mother:	Has he ever tried to kiss you?
Elaine:	Uh huh.
Mother:	You'd better watch it. You're too young to realize it, but things like that can get out of hand.
Elaine:	(leaving the room and busily searching for something to divert her from her mother) I've got to get my hose rinsed out so I'll have some to wear in the morning.

And when a kid gets into trouble, that's when the questions really start to fly—and the communication is more likely to crash and burn. In the following example, Dad just received a phone call from the police. There's been a burglary in the neighborhood and twelve-year-old Eddie (who has broken into houses before) is a prime suspect.

Father:	Eddie, come in here and sit down. I want to have a talk with you.
Eddie:	(complies and sits quietly looking at his father)
Father:	Do you know who that was on the phone?
Eddie:	No.
Father:	It was the police.
Eddie:	(sits quietly, says nothing)
Father:	Do you have anything to say or anything you want to tell me?
Eddie:	No.
Father:	Aren't you even curious about what they had to say?
Eddie:	No.
Father:	Well, a house over on Marion Street was broken into. The only thing they found missing was a bottle of liquor, and there were some vulgar things written on the wall.
Eddie:	So?
Father:	Did you do it? I want you to tell me if you did.
Eddie:	No.
Father:	Can I believe that?
Eddie:	Why not?
Father:	Now tell the truth: we're pretty sure that you did it. You'll make it a lot easier on yourself if you'll just confess, and let us try to get this thing straightened out.
Eddie:	Why are you always on my back? I don't know who broke into that house. You're always blaming me.
Father:	Well, it happened between seven and eight o'clock this evening. Can you account for where you were then?

Eddie: Yeah, I was just out in the neighborhood playing.

Father: Who were you playing with?

Eddie: Oh, Norman and some other kids.

Father: What were you playing?

Eddie: Just Hide and Seek and some other games.

Father: You know I can call Norman's house and ask to talk to him. That way I'll know if you are telling us the truth.

Eddie: Don't go draggin' Norman into this; it's not fair.

Father: Either you admit right now that you did it or I'm going to call Norman and find out. If I have to find out for myself, the punishment is going to be much worse.

Eddie: Okay, I did it! That's what you wanted to hear, isn't it!

Father: Just as I thought. Why in the world do you do things like that?

Eddie: Because it's fun.

Father: How can anything like that be fun?

Eddie: I don't know, I just groove on it. It's exciting, and sometimes I get things I like.

Father: Like liquor, you mean?

Eddie: That's one thing. I give it to Paul (an older boy in the neighborhood). He told me I was really something else for being able to pull off a deal like that.

Father: Have you ever thought of what's going to become of you?

Eddie: No.

Father: How can we get you to stop this?

Eddie: I dunno; electrocute me, I guess.

Father, of course, had more probes than the space program. But by now, you should have some appreciation for the equation PP = PK (probing parents produce passive kids).

Sometimes parents ask questions because they are genuinely interested in their children, and they want to share their experiences. In the next example, Mom's intentions are good, but questions aren't the way to get the intimacy she's trying for:

Mother: (to Larry who is just arriving home from school) Hi, Larry, tell me about your day.

Larry: Oh, it wasn't much.

Mother: Well, what did you do?

Larry: Just went to class and the usual stuff.

Mother: Well, you must have done something interesting or unusual. Did you see anyone or talk to them?

Larry: No.

Mother: I don't know why you're so secretive. You don't ever tell me anything. I get the feeling you don't trust me, or that you just don't like me. Robert tells his mother everything, and they have such nice talks. Why can't you be more like that?

Larry: (in despair) Aw, Mom!

Mom is trying to tell her son that she's interested in him, that she'd like to be close to him, and that she's available if he has anything he'd like to talk about. But you can't demand that a person open up to you unless you're a dentist. You can only create an atmosphere that will allow him to open up. When a person has something important to say, he goes through a process something like peeling an onion. He starts by talking about something relatively superficial. If this layer meets with criticism or probing questions, he will stop peeling. But if he continues to feel safe (you see, we're back to intimacy) then he will go on to the next layer, then the next, and so on until he gets to the heart of the onion, the topic he really wants to discuss.

Now I've told you that you should get close to your children, and that one way to do that is to talk with the child. But then I told you that you shouldn't ask a lot of probing questions. You might now be asking *me* a probing question: "If questions are not the answer, what is? Are we supposed to nod our heads a lot, or what?"

My answer to you is, "You seem to feel a little upset about being told what *not* to do, and you'd like to be told what you *should* do. And I'm not telling you. That's really annoying, isn't it?"

17

Understanding And Reflecting Feelings

Okay, if you're not supposed to ask a lot of questions, then what *are* you supposed to do? I'll let my daughter, Jaye, show you.

Years ago, when she was four years old, Jaye was engaged in her usual inhalation of the evening meal. As she thrashed about at her corner of the table, she overturned a glass of Kool-Aid. We provided a second one. Somehow, our usually dexterous child managed to spill this glass too. There was something special on TV that evening, and Jaye asked to take her drink and dessert into the living room. We granted the request and were rewarded by having her spill the *third* glass. It overturned on the rug, right in front of the TV, just as Mom came into the room. Noting that the rug color and the Kool-Aid did not go at all well together, Mom shrieked in disbelief and grasped her head with both hands. Looking up with a cherubic face, Jaye said, "Just makes you want to scream, doesn't it?"

Jaye had learned something that Carl Rogers, a counseling psychologist, discovered long ago:

Understanding and Reflecting Feelings Facilitates Communication and
Increases Intimacy

Sensing this, Jaye reflected her mother's feelings, not the Sergeant Friday-like "facts" of the situation. By reflecting feelings rather than facts, you will show that you are really listening, *really* trying to understand how the person thinks and feels (not *why* he behaves the way he does). Understanding *why* a person is like he is is called diagnosis (as in, "You've got an oedipal problem" or, "Your mother rejected you and that's why you sleep in your tennis shoes").

Let's look at another example. Suppose that your best friend tells you, "I've just gotten a call from my brother. He says that my mother is in the hospital and she's going to have an operation. They think it's cancer." This message conveys feeling as well as facts. Which part of the message do you respond to? You could say, "Oh, you've gotten a phone call? Wonderful thing, the telephone. Why, if it weren't for Alexander Graham Bell, it would take days to get that news." Or you could focus on another part of the message and say, "Gee, you must be worried sick." The first response deals with a rather unimportant part of the friend's message and shows incredible insensitivity. The second response deals with a more important fact, and it focuses on the other person's feelings and not on those of the listener.

Empathy, like love and telegrams, is of little value unless communicated. It must be experienced by a child. Some listeners are fond of saying, "I understand." But, in doing so, they are in essence asking the speaker to take their word for it. The good parent will *demonstrate* his understanding, thus allowing the child to feel understood. To do this we obviously must say something back. As a rule of thumb, the empathizer should keep his comments brief. He should try to crystallize the main feeling of the speaker in his own words, to re-phrase what was said. Or, the listener can question: "Are you saying . . . . ?" or "Am I understanding you right that. . . . ?" This process, called reflecting feelings, should not be confused with parroting. Parroting is simply repeating back the content of what is said. This is illustrated in a conversation between a teenager and a novice parental empathizer. It illustrates what *not* to do, namely parrot back words rather than reflecting feelings:

Teenager: I've had it.
Parent: You've had it.
Teenager: I'm at the end of my rope.
Parent: I see, you're at the end of your rope.
Teenager: I just can't take it anymore.
Parent: You can't take it anymore.
Teenager: Yes, but what's wrong with the way I say it?

Reflecting feelings doesn't mean parroting what someone says. It means getting at the core of what he says and showing that you understand the feelings he's trying to express. In the last chapter I showed you how asking questions can inhibit communication and intimacy. Now, let's look at those same examples and see how reflecting feelings can facilitate communication and increase intimacy.

Nancy, you recall, had decided she'd prefer to skip her operation. If Dad had been listening to feelings instead of facts, the conversation might have gone this way:

Nancy: Daddy, I've decided I don't want to have the operation.
Father: It sounds like you're getting a little frightened.
Nancy: Yes, more than just a little. I don't know if I can stand it much longer.
Father: You mean you'd like to hurry up and get this over with?
Nancy: Well, I wish it were over, but I don't want to hurry it up. I wish I could forget it altogether.
Father: I know how it is when you're afraid. You want to get it over with and at the same time you want to get away from it.
Nancy: Boy, is that right! I keep remembering how Mary Anne went to the hospital that time. She went to sleep and never woke up.
Father: And you can't help wondering if the same thing might happen to you?
Nancy: Yeah!
Father: I can see this has scared you a lot more than any of us realized.

Nancy: I just can't hold it back anymore (begins to sob).

Father: (comes closer to the daughter and allows her to cry on his shoulder)

Nancy: You won't let anything happen to me, will you?

Father: I'll do everything I can to make sure things come out right. We've gotten you the best doctor and the best hospital. And I'll stay here with you if you need me.

Nancy: Will that make everything come out okay?

Father: You want to know if I really believe that everything is going to be all right?

Nancy: Yes.

Father: I honestly believe it will.

Nancy: (giving a slight smile) Be sure you're here when I go in and when I wake up from the operation.

Father: I will.

Nancy: Good.

Father: You seem to be feeling a little better now.

Nancy: I am.

Similarly, instead of playing amateur detective, Eddie's father might have handled a tough situation better if he had listened to feelings:

Father: Eddie, come here; I want to talk to you a minute.

Eddie: Okay.

Father: That was the police on the phone. They said a house over on Marion Street was broken into and they think you're the one who did it.

Eddie: Well, I didn't.

Father: They asked if I would talk to you and see if I could find out the facts, rather than them doing it.

Eddie: There's nothing to find out.

Father: You seem to be pretty irritated about this whole deal.

Eddie: Wouldn't you if you were always being accused of something?

Father: So, you're mad because you're being accused of something you didn't do?

Eddie: Right! You got it.

Father: Well, the police seem to feel they have some evidence that indicates that you did it. If you confess, there'll be a meeting with the court counselor, but no court appearance provided you pay for the damage done. If you don't confess they say there will be an inquiry and possibly a trial.

Eddie: Why is everybody always picking on me? Are you going to let them do that?

Father: Yes, I'm not going to interfere with the police doing their job, even when it involves my own family.

Eddie: The easiest thing would be to say I did it whether I really did or not.

Father: You seem to feel trapped, even willing to admit a crime you didn't commit in order to get out.

Eddie: No, I *did* do it.

Father: I was afraid of that, but I'm glad you've owned up to it, rather than making the situation worse.

Eddie: What happens now?

Father: You seem scared.

Eddie: (crying) Yes, what are they going to do to me?

Father: We'll have to go in at ten o'clock on Saturday morning. The counselor will explain to you that you will be allowed to pay for having the house repaired. He'll probably also tell you that this is the last mistake you can make without being taken into court, tried, and sentenced.

Eddie: Are you going to be there on Saturday morning?

Father: Yes, I'm required to be there too. You sound like you'd rather I weren't.

Eddie: Yes, I'd rather just go by myself.

Father: It seems like you're ashamed and you would like as few people to know about this as possible.

Eddie: Right. Who are you going to tell?

Father: I won't tell anyone but your mother.

Notice that Eddie's father did not change his own position. Understanding how Eddie feels does not mean joining him in a crime by covering for him, nor does it mean condoning what he did. And Father's understanding does not get Eddie off the hook. But it does let Eddie know that his father cares, and brings him closer to his father, whereas questions only drove them apart.

Many parents want their children to confess, because, as parents, they are so lacking in self-confidence that they can't bring themselves to punish unless the child admits his guilt. Although it is commendable to avoid unjust punishment, we do not serve the child's best interest by leading him to think that he can get away with murder if: (1) he can keep from confessing, or (2) he isn't informed of his rights before he does so. In the final analysis, the role of parent is more akin to that of a referee in a sporting event than to a Justice of the Supreme Court. After all, most parental decisions are judgment calls. All parents misjudge from time to time, but they *must* make a decision. It is the insecure parent who is most likely to feel he must have a confession in hand before he can "get a conviction" and proceed with the matter of punishment. Parents should take the attitude that they not only can, but must, act on their opinion. Granted, they will sometimes be wrong, but it is a waste of time to argue with the child about who is right. They should simply state that, as parents, they must act on their opinion, while allowing the child to believe whatever he must about whether the parent is right or wrong. This may, on rare occasions, result in a child being punished inappropriately. It may sometimes cause one child to be punished when, in fact another child was at fault. Nonetheless, parents are obligated to follow their better judgment.

Some parents are afraid to empathize because they feel it is too much like agreeing with a child. Empathizing, however, does not remove the parent from his responsibility to set limits and provide rewards and punishments. It is generally best if one empathizes first, assures the child that he is understood, and then sets and enforces the limits as necessary. The chances are that the punishment will have a more desirable effect if the child feels understood and his defenses are thus lowered. The reason why most parents are not understood, and the reason why words of any kind are of so little value in childrearing is that children simply do not listen and hear objectively. The best way to alter this situation, and to maximize the chance that we will really communicate with our child, is to earn the right to be heard. The only way to do that is to listen and understand the child from his point of view. If we demand that the child understand us, without our having understood him, we are likely to find that our pearls of wisdom are falling upon little deaf ears.

If Larry's mom (in the last chapter) had matched her good intentions with skill at reflecting feelings, she would have gotten the intimacy she sought:

Larry: (age seven, enters house and goes quietly to his room)

Mother: (noting that the son is home but hasn't greeted anyone, goes to his room) Hi, Larry, I see you're home. You came in so quietly I didn't know for sure if you were here or not.

Larry: (looks at the floor) Where are my crayons?

Mother: The last time I saw them they were in your brother's room. I think he has been using them. (then empathically) Something seems to be bothering you.

Larry: (doesn't say anything and leaves to search for crayons)

Mother: (allows Larry to leave but doesn't follow; he then returns to the room with crayons) Something really does seem to be bothering you, but you don't act like you want to talk about it.

Larry: (looks down, shakes his head "No" and says nothing and begins to color)

Mother: Well, that's fine. If you *do* decide to talk about it, let me know. (she then gives Larry an affectionate hug)

Larry: (raises up in bed, hugs mother closely and begins to cry)

Mother: Something is really bothering you. It looks to me like you need to talk about it.

Larry: I had an accident today at school.

Mother: You mean you wet your pants?

Larry: Yeah, during the spelling bee.

Mother: (holding him closely) That must have been embarrassing. I'm so sorry.

Larry: (says nothing)

Mother: (picking up on the non-verbal cues) You're probably wondering if people will forget, and if everything will ever be all right again.

Larry: (feeling better, begins to breathe a little deeper, stops crying and even manages a meager smile)

Larry's *feelings* about wetting his pants are much more important than the objective facts. Many parents would be inclined to say things like, "It's really not important," or "It happens to all children," or, "One day you'll look back on this experience and laugh." The child is likely to respond to these incredible "insights" by saying "You don't understand," and he would be right—if you say things like that you're not really listening, you're not trying to understand how the child *feels*. Whether or not the event will one day seem trivial is beside the point: the fact is that right now the child feels like hell. You either understand that or you don't. And if you do understand it, you'll show it by reflecting feelings.

Some parents must understand and reflect a child's feelings, even though sometimes, to an adult, those feelings may seem trivial. There are no trivial feelings, though some feelings are more important than others.

Some of the most important feelings a person has are about me.

18

Feeling Good About Me

Me is the name we give ourselves, and we're a lot better off if we like the person who carries that name.

Some of the most important feelings a person has are feelings about himself, about what kind of person he is. For example, in the last chapter, Larry felt badly about wetting his pants in school. Events like that are embarrassing, but they also make a child miserable because they affect how he feels about himself: "Am I a bedwetter? Am I a baby? The other kids don't wet their pants; what's wrong with me?"

If you've read *The Death of a Salesman*, you'll remember that Willy Loman's feelings about himself changed for the worse when he was no longer able to be the hot-shot salesman he had been, which meant that he was no longer a good provider. As a result, he started to spend more and more of his time thinking about and talking about the old days—when he had felt better about himself. His suicide was a way of redeeming what he considered his lost self-esteem: his life insurance made him a good provider again. Obviously, Willy's suicide was not a healthy thing to do, but it was his way of trying to feel worthwhile.

Several authors have pointed out the relationship between adaptive behavior on the one hand and thinking well of ourselves on the other. Norman Vincent Peale (*The Power of Positive Thinking*) and Maxwell Maltz (*Psychocybernetics and Self Fulfillment*) are two such writers. Their books, would lead us to think that one can brainwash or "psych" himself into feeling adequate. The fact is, however, that even though we can usually talk ourselves into *thinking* we are adequate, this will have little or no effect on our visceral or gut *feelings* of adequacy. If we have only mentally sold ourselves on our own adequacy, these feelings may desert us when we enter a challenging situation.

The basic principle is that:

People Need To Feel Good About Themselves

How a child feels about himself, how he defines himself, depends to a large extent upon how his parents define him. Take the following incident, for example:

Janice: Rob took an ice pick and stuck it in my bike tire.

Father: What's gotten into that kid? Just wait till I get my hands on him! Rob! Get yourself in here right now. What's this I hear about you poking an ice pick in Janice's tire? The very idea!

Rob: (age eight, enters, trembling, with head down, but doesn't say anything)

Father: You look at me, young man.

Rob: (looks up)

Father: (shaking his finger in his son's face) I ought to beat you within an inch of your life. Don't you ever do anything like that again. The very idea of deliberately sticking an ice pick in a bicycle tire. Go get me a yardstick.

Rob: (obeys the command and returns with the yardstick)

Father: (jerks the child toward him by the arm, hitting him several times with extremely hard licks)

Rob: (cries bitterly)

Father: Are you ever going to do anything like that again?

Rob: (sobs and cries)

Father: (angrily) Answer me! Are you ever going to do anything like that again?

Rob: No.

Father: Things like this may be the first step on the way to reform school. A kid of eight who's sticking an ice pick in a bicycle tire will probably be sticking a knife into people by the time he's grown up.

Instead of focusing on what Rob did and responding to that behavior appropriately, Rob's father defines the boy as a miniature Machine Gun Kelly. What Rob did was wrong, and Father should certainly not condone such behavior, but it's the *behavior* that should be discouraged, not the *child*. If the father persists in attributing negative definitions to Rob, the boy will soon believe them. And once he believes them himself, he will act in accordance with them. In other words, the father's name-calling tactics are likely to perpetuate, not discourage, the unwanted behavior. This episode could have been dealt with effectively without making Rob feel that he was N.D.G. (No Damn Good).

Janice: Rob took an ice pick and stuck it in my bike tire.

Father: Wow! I thought he knew better than that. Where is he?

Janice: He's in the next room.

Father: (enters the room, rather than venting his rage on the child by ordering him to come forth) I hear you stuck an ice pick in Janice's bike tire.

Rob: Well, she made me mad.

Father: (taking the occasion to empathize rather than vent his own anger) Whatever she did must have really made you angry.

Rob: I just asked her to let me ride her bike up to the store. She's so selfish she wouldn't let me do it.

Father: I know selfishness can really get to you sometimes.

Rob: She's just a snot-nosed little brat. But I showed her.

Father: Well, I'm going to have to punish you. You get her bicycle fixed at your own expense and pay her a dollar for every day she has to be without it.

Rob: But it's six blocks to the service station and the bike won't roll.

Father: I think you can probably get it there by lifting one wheel and rolling on the other. But, if that's too much work, I'd be willing to run it up there for you for a dollar and a half.

Rob: But I don't have a dollar and a half.

Father: Well, I'll give you twenty-five cents for sweeping the garage and you can sweep it six times, say on Saturday, for the next six weeks. That way you can earn the money.

Rob: I think I'll roll it.

Father: Fine. When everything is taken care of, you'll be even with the world again.

This time Father rejects Rob's behavior, rather than Rob and uses correction (see chapter eleven) to discourage that kind of behavior from being repeated. But in this example, Rob is still Rob, he hasn't metamorphosed into some kind of werewolf.

Another way that parents can undermine a child's esteem is to continually focus on minor failings:

Father: (to eight-year-old son who has just made a brief appearance in a Little League baseball game) I can't believe what you did out there. You walked four straight batters!

Ralph: (looks down, remains quiet)

Father: You threw sixteen straight outside pitches. It seems to me if you throw a ball outside a dozen times in a row, you might try throwing it inside, in hopes that it would go over the plate.

Ralph: (continues to look down, says nothing)

Father: Can't you at least answer me?

Ralph: What do you want me to say?

Father: I want to know what you think about it.

Ralph: About what?

Father: (in exasperation) Oh, I give up!

Now, it's probably safe to assume that Ralph did not deliberately walk four batters in a row, and it is probably also safe to assume that he feels pretty rotten about his performance. The only thing Father accomplishes with his criticism is to confirm Ralph's suspicions that he is a worthless ball player and a lousy human being. Now if Father had been thinking about his son, he might have reflected Ralph's feelings:

Father: You seem kind of down.

Ralph: (nods his head)

Father: You're disappointed that you didn't pitch better?

Ralph: (again nods yes)

Father: You look like it's *really* got you down.

Ralph: Oh, I'll get over it eventually.

Father: (jokingly) You don't think you'll have any lasting scars?
Ralph: I don't think so.
Father: Glad to hear you say that. It bothers me to see you so disappointed.

Some parents can pick more than a coal miner:
Mother: Myron, your nose is running again; take care of it right now.
Myron: (age eight) Sniff.
Mother: And sit up straight. You're always slouching around. I swear, you've developed the worst posture. I wouldn't be surprised if you don't have trouble with your back when you get older; besides, it looks terrible.
Myron: (makes a meager attempt to assume a better sitting position)
Mother: And pull in your stomach.
Myron: (continues eating his supper, but says nothing)
Mother: Do you have to make so much noise? That smacking is about to drive me out of my mind, and you have some corn on your cheek clear around by your ear. Use your napkin!
Myron: (wipes his face, but his expression betrays feelings of both guilt and sadness) Can I have my dessert now?
Mother: Yes, I'm getting it. Don't be so impatient.
Myron: (says nothing, but seems anxious)
Mother: (getting up to get dessert) Will you stop that fidgeting? You just wiggle and fidget all the time. It bugs me.
Myron: (now looks like a "whipped pup")
Mother: Now don't get that look on your face; just straighten up and act right.

I'll admit that little Myron is not Emily Post's idea of perfection, but the poor kid may as well have Don Rickles as a mother. Mom's message to Myron comes in the constant rapid-fire of a machine gun: you do not measure up, you are N.D.G.

Parents are the most important people around when it comes to a child's feelings about himself. But other people can have important effects: teachers, grandparents, other children. A child's brothers and sisters can have powerful influence on a child's self image. A parent should be on the watch for demeaning comments by other members of the family:
Leonard: (eleven-year-old) Mom, look at Patty (five-year-old sister). Look at how she's coloring the picture of the President. She gave him an orange coat! (laughs hysterically) And a pink tie! (laughs even louder) And would you believe green shoes! (now rolling on the floor and holding his stomach) Boy, what a retardate! I can't believe anybody is so dumb.
Patty: (who *is* having some trouble learning in the first grade) Mama, make him shut up. Make him quit bothering me.
Mother: (fifteen minutes later) Leonard, come here in the bedroom and help me scoot this chest back in place.
Leonard: (entering room) What chest, Mom?
Mother: Wait a minute and let me close the door.

90

Leonard: (looks at his mother inquisitively)

Mother: I didn't call you in about the chest. I want to ask you to help me do something which I think is very important, but which I don't think you understand. Patty does have some difficulty in learning certain things, although she seems quite bright in other ways. Now, how she feels about herself is extremely important. It would be a *real* shame if Patty began to feel that she were dumb. It would take a lot of happiness away from her and probably make her less able to learn. This is why I want you to help her to feel good about herself. You're her older brother and you probably don't realize it, but what you think and say is really important to her. Anytime you say something like "You're dumb," part of that soaks in, even though she may not let on like it does. I don't want you to call her "dumb" or do anything else that would make her feel as though she weren't bright. Right now, I'm just asking you, and I think you're old enough and concerned enough to help out. If you forget or if you choose not to cooperate, I'll have to make a rule about saying things like that, and punish you if you break it. Do you understand what I'm saying?

Leonard: Yeah.

Mother: Good. I'm sure I can count on you.

A child's feelings are very important. But children are not the only ones in the house with feelings.

19

Nobody Likes A Phony

Although some children might argue the point, I am personally convinced that parents, too, have feelings. And parents' feelings sometimes cause a lot of trouble. This is because parents often violate the principle of congruence, which says that:

A Parent's Behavior and Feelings Should Be Consistent

In simple language, this means that parents should not be hypocrites. To be congruent is to be genuine, sincere, honest Nobody likes a phony, but unfortunately, many parents are about as genuine as an undertaker's grief. They are simply too distant or aloof.

Sometimes parents are incongruent (phony) when they try to get close to a child:

Father: (coming home from work) Hi, champ, how's my little slugger today?
Dirk: (age seven) Hello, Father.
Father: Slayed any dragons lately?
Dirk: No, Father.
Father: What do you mean no? Is that any way for the next Olympic fencing champion to talk? Okay, run out and play so I can visit with your mother.

Father thinks he's being friendly, but he's really being phony, and also rather clumsy. This sort of phoniness is so common, I want to give you another example:

Dad: (observing his son walking sleepily to the breakfast table) How's my little man?
Kirk: (no comment)
Dad: I bet my little lumberjack is ready for a big breakfast.
Kirk: I'm too sleepy to eat.
Dad: You'll never grow up to be a professional football player if you talk like that.

What these parents say to their kids is about as genuine as a Hollywood set. Worse yet, Dirk and Kirk are being treated like objects or toys, not like people. These fathers are also being phony in that they are trying to manipulate their sons: Dirk's father wants him out of the way so he can talk to the mother, and Kirk's father wants him to eat his breakfast. Both dads think they are using psychology, and you can practically smell their smugness. Kids go along with this kind of phoniness, but that doesn't mean that they fall for it.

Sometimes parents are incongruent because they want to support their child. The child who is not so smart will come to realize his limitations and live with them. But what does he do if he has a parent saying things like, "What do you mean you don't think you can make it to college? Of course you're going to go to college. Now stop talking nonsense." The parent may think he's being supportive, but he may only be making his child feel more inadequate. Cindy is a sixteen-year-old girl with a slightly deformed leg that causes her to limp:

Cindy: Mom, I sure wish someone would ask me to the prom.

Mother: Someone will ask you, just you wait and see.

Cindy: Well, no one has yet, and I don't think anyone's going to.

Mother: Yes, they are.

Cindy: No one would want to ask a cripple.

Mother: Don't say the word "cripple." You are *not* crippled. Don't ever let me hear you say that again. You are *not* crippled.

Cindy: I wonder if I'll ever get married.

Mother: Well, of course you'll get married, and it won't be too long now. One of these days someone's going to come along and sweep you off your feet. It will be the most wonderful thing in the world.

It's amazing how much more willing kids sometimes are to accept their own limitations than their parents are. In this example, Mom insists that Cindy will be asked to the prom and that she will marry someday. Now, how does she know that? Has she been taking ESP lessons? And then Mom objects to Cindy using the word "cripple." Well, it's true that Cindy is a lot of things, and shouldn't think of herself *only* in terms of a handicap (see chapter six in the appendix for more on this) but Mom's loud protest makes it clear that the handicap is very important, something to worry about.

Incongruence causes trouble because it undermines a parent's credibility. If parents are dishonestly supportive, then how can a child believe them when they offer sincere support? Mom could have been genuine and still offered support:

Cindy: I wish someone would ask me to the prom.

Mother: I know that's distressing. I know how much you'd like to go, and yet you have to wait for someone to ask you.

Cindy: That's right. The boys can just ask anyone, but girls have to wait around and hope someone will ask them.

Mother: That's one place where women really get the worst end of the deal.

Cindy: Besides, what boy would want to ask a cripple anyway?

Mother: I guess at your age, the problem with your leg bothers you more than it ever has before.

Cindy: I'd give anything if I were just like the other girls.

Mother: I wish everything were just as you wanted it.

Cindy: Oh, Mom, you're so sweet.

Mother: You're nice to say that.

Cindy: But I wonder if I'm ever going to get married.

Mother: So that's part of the worry, too. I guess that adds to your concern about the prom.

Cindy: Yes, I think about it a lot. But I see a lot of other women who aren't perfect physically, and a lot of them seem to have nice husbands. I just hope I will too.

Mother: So do I, if that's what you want.

You'll notice that, in this example, Mom has read the chapter on reflecting feelings very carefully. But she's also genuine.

Another way that incongruence gets parents into trouble is in disciplining a child. The parent may *say* one thing, but mean something else. Sometimes a parent says "yes" when he means "no," "stop" when he means "go," and "that's good" when he means "that's bad." For example, when someone shouts, "I AM *NOT* ANGRY!" we know that he is incongruent, and also angry. And when a parent scolds a child for some misconduct, but does it in a way that shows her delight, she is being incongruent:

Mother: (to Travis, age eight) Now, don't go acting too big for your britches. There are rules at the pool, safety rules. Don't you run, and don't get up on the fifteen-foot diving board.

Travis: (says nothing, but displays a somewhat fiendish-looking grin)

Mother: (becomes preoccupied with a card game at poolside then looks and sees Travis on the fifteen-foot board)

Travis: (jumps in as soon as mother is watching)

Mother: (beckons Travis to come over, then in the presence of other adults says) Did you see what this little man did? He jumped the whole fifteen feet. Why, there are kids twice his age who wouldn't do that. Sometimes he just baffles me. What am I going to do with him?

If you recall chapter thirteen, you'll notice that mother is actually rewarding behavior that she would probably insist she is punishing. Similarly, Mrs. Casey complains that she has tried everything to make Gretchen stop using four-letter words, but then says with a grin, "What am I going to do with that little devil?" Obviously, Mrs. Casey gets a kick out of her daughter's rakish behavior.

In the following example, Brent, age fifteen, is guilty of having taken the family car without permission. Brent's father is sure of his guilt, but tries to hide his suspicion and manipulate Brent into admitting his guilt.

Father: Where were you yesterday evening about five o'clock? I called home and no one was here.

Brent: Outside, I guess.

Father: What were you up to?

Brent: Just messing around with the guys.

Father: What do you do when you mess around with the guys?

Brent: Oh, nothing; just talk.

Father: How have things been going lately?

Brent: Fine.

Father: Have you been getting into any trouble?

Brent: No.

Father: Well, is there anything that you want to tell me?

Brent: No, why do you ask?

Father: I just thought you might have something you'd like to get off your chest.

Brent: No.

Father: Bill Johnson from down the street said he saw someone who looked like you drive by his house last night.

Brent: Far out!

Brent seems to have learned his lessons in counter-manipulation well. When the father is indirect, Brent becomes as innocent and passive as a snowflake. He doesn't let Dad maneuver him into a corner; he doesn't even dignify his father's accusations with so much as a direct denial. The father could have obtained better results if he had been honest about his feelings and had acted on them.

Father: Mr. Johnson told me he saw you driving the car.

Brent: I didn't take the car.

Father: Well, I'm forced to think that you did take it because of what Mr. Johnson told me.

Brent: He must have seen somebody else. I didn't take it.

Father: That would be awfully strange, Mr. Johnson just dreaming up something like that.

Brent: But I didn't do it.

Father: Well, I'm not convinced that you *didn't* take the car, and yet I don't know for sure that you *did*. But I've got to go on what I *believe* to be true. If I'm wrong, I'm sorry.

Brent: It's not fair.

Father: If you're innocent, you're right: it isn't fair. But for me to do nothing, when my belief is that you *did* do it, would be irresponsible.

Being honest about one's feelings can also provide your child with good feedback about his behavior. If nobody bothers to tell Karen that belching is no longer considered cute after about age two, then she may continue to do it for an embarrassingly long time. Why not tell her that it puts you off? And if you learn to say to your teenager, "What you did makes me boil inside," he may change his behavior *before* you explode in righteous wrath.

The one thing which makes congruence a MUST is that, unless we verbalize our negative feelings toward our own children, these feelings come out in other ways. This is as certain as death and taxes. Let me illustrate: A former patient of mine and her four-year-old daughter displayed real creative genius in their ability to antagonize one another. Little Charlotte was a walking Geiger counter when it came to finding things that would upset her mother, and she could do them in the most innocent fashion. For instance, when the first flowers came up in the spring, she would gather them and bring them to her mother, but before their time to be picked. This, of course, made the mother angry, yet she found it difficult to express her anger since Charlotte gave the outward appearance of performing an act of affection. Charlotte also got a lot of mileage out of mud puddles. If there was one within four hundred yards of the house, she could always find it and "accidentally" fall in. Once when Charlotte had gotten muddy, the mother seemed to be trying to control her rage by denying it. Perhaps she was afraid she might lose complete control if she gave *any* expression to her anger. So Mother forced a chuckle, and proceeded to use what she mistakenly called "psychology" on Charlotte. "Just look how dirty you've gotten," she said. "Now you have to go to all the work of changing your clothes. Go to the bedroom and put on some clean ones." Ten minutes later, Charlotte emerged from the bedroom in clean clothes, but accidentally bumped a bookcase causing a book to fall. At this point the mother grabbed the child and shook her, screaming, "What are you trying to do, tear the house down?" The mother had not expressed her anger directly and honestly, so, ten minutes later, it came out in conjunction with an apparently innocent collision with a bookcase. Under these conditions, Charlotte might have come to feel that getting dirty was a minor crime, but that she would be held without bail if she ever nudged another bookcase.

The more straightforward, honest, and accurate the feedback a child gets from his parents, the better the child will develop. One reason that children learn quickly about their physical environment is that, unlike people, other aspects of the environment are never incongruent. A hot stove always burns, and because of this children learn quickly to be careful around hot stoves.

Unless, of course, their parents are in the cavalry.

20

Parents And The Cavalry

When I was a kid, I used to spend a lot of my Saturday afternoons at the movies, watching the cavalry charge triumphantly to the rescue of settlers who had gotten themselves into another mess. You always knew that no matter what sort of trouble the settlers got themselves into, no matter how stupidly the wagon master behaved, no matter how formidable the odds, the cavalry would rush in at the last minute and save the day. After a few years of getting saved by the army, the settlers might be expected to get careless. Why, they probably wouldn't even bother forming the wagons in a circle at night; they'd let their guards fall asleep; they'd trespass on sacred Indian territory. I figure that they knew they could get away with murder because the cavalry was only a few frames away.

Some parents are like the cavalry. They hover over the child. They're constantly lurking in the background, ready to rush in to the rescue at the critical moment. What they don't realize is that they are preventing the child's learning from his own experience. They prevent the child from learning the natural benefits and consequences of his own behavior. Many parents unwisely expend a major effort to prevent their children from suffering pain or disappointment. This is more often true for those of us who may have suffered bitter experiences as children. The idea is a good one when it applies to bad experiences or exploitation imposed on the child by others, but it is a horse of a different color when it prevents children from making their own mistakes. This privilege is not a luxury, but an essential ingredient for the growth of a sense of responsibility. It will not occur if children are not allowed to make bad, or pain producing, decisions. Neither can it be accomplished if parents let the child off, or bail him out, if he gets into trouble outside the home.

If there is a single concept which best distinguishes an effective from an ineffective parent it is this. A poor parent is one who intervenes between a child's behavior and the consequences of that behavior. A good parent is one who allows a child to experience the consequences of his acts.

That may sound harsh, but the fact is that the world provides its own rewards and punishments, and sooner or later the child has to deal with those himself; he cannot rely upon Mom and Dad to come to the rescue all of the time. Now, this does not mean that you should stand by mutely as your four-year-old consumes every colorful tablet in the medicine cabinet, and then, as the child slips into a coma, say, "I guess *that'll* teach you a lesson." That would be carrying things to an extreme. But so many parents go to the opposite extreme. The child plays carelessly with a toy and breaks it? Mom buys him a new one. He leaves his bicycle out in the rain to rust? Dad will clean it up for him. Pretty soon the child is behaving like the Saturday afternoon settlers, not bothering to put his wagons in a circle, falling asleep on guard duty, trespassing on sacred Indian territory. Mom or Dad always come to the rescue.

What inevitably happens is that Mom and Dad complain about the child's irresponsibility, "You never take care of anything," "You have no regard for property." Well, these accusations are undoubtedly true. But who taught the child to be this way? The cavalry.

The principle that I'm leading up to is the principle of responsibility:

Every Child Must Learn To Accept The Consequences Of His Own Behavior

Being an adult means being responsible. But people do not automatically become responsible as they grow older. They become responsible because as they get older, they are expected to accept the consequences for their behavior. If a nine-month-old baby throws a wooden block out of his crib and hits someone with it, no one feels that the baby has behaved irresponsibly. But when a child is four years old, he should know that such behavior will not be tolerated.

Taking on increasing responsibility is actually rather rewarding, and most kids get a bang out of being responsible. But parents sometimes get in the way; they refuse to let the child become responsible. They monitor the child's every act. They tell him when he has eaten too much, and when he hasn't eaten enough. They make sure that he is dressed warmly enough, that his clothes are color coordinated. A father who spent his money on an old worn-out car when he was a teenager may not allow his son to buy an old jalopy.

When Harry gets mad, he usually picks up something and threatens to throw it through a window. His mother always restrains him, reasons with him and occasionally spanks him. Harry's playmate Kurt thought this looked like fun, so he tried it out the next time he and his mother got into it. Kurt picked up a baseball and threatened to throw it through a sliding glass door. His mother failed to follow the script. She didn't rush in to stop him as he expected. Kurt hadn't thought out beforehand what to do in this event, so he threw the baseball and broke the window. For the next twenty-five weeks, Kurt's dollar allowance went to pay for the repair of the window. Kurt learned a lot from this experience, and hasn't tried to manipulate his mother into taking responsibility for his behavior again. Meanwhile, Harry's mother is still holding him back. Harry's mother is still playing the cavalry, taking responsibility for the foolishness of the settlers.

Some parents feel that they are not meeting their own responsibility as a parent if they do not prevent their child from behaving unwisely. "What would the teachers say if Imogene came to school in the winter without a coat? They'd think she had a terrible mother." But the parent who feels truly responsible will be able to do what is in the best interest of his children, regardless of what the neighbors or someone else may think.

Sometimes parents allow a child's distress to discourage them from imposing responsibility. Take for example the case of Len, who is dillydallying about getting ready for school:

Mother: Len, you'd better get ready; you're going to be late for your bus.

Len: (continues to dillydally and says nothing)

Mother: Len, you'd better get going; you're going to miss your bus.

Len: (continues to delay)

Mother: Len, it's 7:50. The bus will be at the corner in five minutes, and you aren't even dressed yet. Now get with it.

Len: (leaves the breakfast table and goes to his room)

Mother: (goes to Len's room) Is that all the dressing you've done? Here, let me help you get your socks on! Let me tie your shoe! You're too slow!

Len: (complies but says nothing)

Mother: Let that shoe go. You'll just have to leave with it untied.

Len: Aw, Mom.

Mother: Now, get out of here.

Len: (leaves)

Mother: Len, you've forgotten your coat. Here, put this hand here. I swear, you don't seem to be able to do anything. (Mother opens door and rushes Len out)

The way Len's mom took over made Hitler look like he was only borrowing Poland. Had Len missed the bus, she undoubtedly would have taken him to school. Not only does she usurp his sense of responsibility, but she may also create feelings of inadequacy or self-doubt by, in effect, telling him he can't do anything on his own. A more skilled parent would have reacted more like this:

Mother: Len, I don't know if you're watching the time or not, but it's ten minutes until your bus gets here. I'm not going to say anymore about it.

Len: (dillydallying at the breakfast table)

Mother: You seem upset about something this morning.

Len: I am. Mrs. Frederick's an old witch.

Mother: You're mad at her, and that's why you aren't getting with it?

Len: She made me write, "I will not talk in class" one hundred times.

Mother: I didn't see you writing that.

Len: Well, I haven't written it yet.

Mother: And you're a little afraid to go to school without it.

Len: I hate her and I'm not going back.

Mother: Well, you will have to go to school, and if you miss the bus you'll have to walk.

Len: I won't walk. I just won't go to school.

Mother: If you don't go to school, that's breaking the law. I'll have to report you, and you'll have to take the consequences.

Len: (continues to dillydally but says nothing)

Mother: Well, I just saw the bus go by, so you've missed it.

Len: (says nothing)

Mother: (although tempted to give in because Len is upset, decides to do nothing at this point and in the spirit of responsibility leaves the next move to Len)

Len: (ten minutes later appears with his cap on) Will you take me to school?

Mother: No. I hate for you to have to walk. But I'm not willing to take you, since you decided on your own to miss the bus.

Len: Well, I'm going to be late.

Mother: I know you can't walk that mile and a half and get there on time, but at least the consequences of being tardy aren't as bad as not getting there at all.

Len: You mean you're really going to make me walk?

Mother: Yes.

Len: (leaves the house weeping silently to himself)

Mother: (touched by the tears, but does not intervene except to say) I'm really sorry you feel so badly. I know this is hard on you. I'll see you this afternoon, and I hope things are better then.

Sometimes children like the idea of having a pet, and a pet can be an excellent way for a child to learn to accept responsibility—if the parents are willing to really make the child responsible. Twelve-year-old Wanda's father can't get out of the habit of assuming responsibility for her:

Wanda: Dad, can I buy a dog? I was down at Trade Mart, and they had this cute little black and white terrior. It's eight months old and only costs five dollars.

Father: That's the silliest thing I ever heard: five dollars for a mutt. Absolutely not. Besides, is it a male or a female?

Wanda: I don't know for sure, but I think it's a female.

Father: See there, you don't even know anything about what you're doing. You don't even know whether it's a male or a female or what the implications are if you get a female. There'll be all those puppies, and a dog in heat, and the males hanging around. Besides it would be a lot of work for all of us, cleaning up the messes and things like that. I'm just not going to have it.

Wanda: You never let me do anything around here!

Father: One of these days you'll thank me.

If father had been interested in teaching his daughter responsibility, the conversation would have gone more like this:

Wanda: Dad, can I have a dog?

Father: Sure, Wanda, you can have anything you're capable of assuming the responsibility for.

Wanda: Well, I want to buy this eight-month-old dog that I saw at Trade Mart.

Father: Is your mind made up or are you asking for advice?

Wanda: My mind's made up.

Father: That's fine, but you'll be responsible for buying food and feeding the dog, cleaning up any messes or damage he does to the furniture and rugs, paying the vet bills, and so forth. In other words, everything.

Wanda: That's fine.

"That's fine," you may agree, "as long as things work out all right. But if things don't, who gets left holding the leash?" If Father really believes in giving Wanda responsibility, "she" does. Let's suppose that Wanda returns home that evening with a small eight-month-old terrior. The dog is placed in the garage where it cries all night. Wanda is forced to turn her bedroom (where the dog cannot be heard) over to her parents and she has to move into their room.

Over a period of several weeks, Wanda is burdened with the cost of dog food, the cleaning of the garage, and having to feed "Sugar." Eventually there is a five dollar assessment for damaged draperies. Finally, Wanda has second thoughts about being a pet owner:

Wanda: I think I want to get rid of Sugar.

Father: It's gotten to be too much for you, hasn't it?

Wanda: Yes.

Father: There are two bulletin boards at work where people put notices of houses to rent, cars to sell and pets to give away. If you'd like, I'll put up a notice.

Wanda: I would.

Father: Type up two, and I'll put one on each bulletin board.

Whether owning a pet is a good idea or not is not the point. The point is that Wanda had the opportunity to make a decision for herself and reap the gains—or suffer the losses. She had the chance to be responsible.

Of course, you can't expect a two-year-old to accept the same kind of responsibilities you'd expect a sixteen-year-old to meet. But when it comes to deciding how much responsibility to give a child, parents generally err in the direction of giving too little, too late. Obviously we do not hold an infant accountable for soiling his diapers, but in the following example, Mother is still accepting responsibility for five-year-old Conrad's natural functions:

Mother: Conrad, go to the bathroom. You're squirming around like a whirling dervish.

Conrad: No!

Mother: Go on. You *do* have to go, don't you?

Conrad: No!

Mother: Well, go anyway.

Conrad: I don't want to!

Mother: Now go before you have an accident.

Conrad: I'm going to get a hatchet and chop you up.

Mother: Why Conrad, that's a terrible thing to say. You wouldn't want to hurt me, would you?

Conrad: Yes.

Mother: Now this is silly. You march yourself into the bathroom right this instant.

Now, I ask you, who knows better than Conrad when Conrad has to go to the bathroom? Conrad's mom seems to think *she* does! She is trying to take responsibility for seeing to it that Conrad gets to the bathroom when necessary. But Conrad is toilet trained, he knows when and how to use the bathroom, and he doesn't require any coaching. The situation would have been better handled if the parent had put the responsibility where it belonged—with Conrad. At the most, she might have reminded him of his responsibilities:

Mom: Conrad, you're squirming around a lot as though you need to use the bathroom.

Conrad: I don't need to go to the bathroom!

Mom: Fine. Just remember that if you use your pants as a toilet, you will have to wash them out.

This time Mother makes Conrad responsible for his own behavior.

The goal of the parent is to shift more and more responsibility from themselves to the child, to do less and less so that by age seventeen or eighteen the child is able to handle adult responsibilities. It should be a gradual, steady transition from childhood to adulthood. If parents persist in taking responsibilities that ought to be turned over to the child, then after seventeen or eighteen years of hard labor, they will be the parents of a very old baby. It is a mistake to think that you can come running in like the cavalry, protecting the child from every hardship, and then suddenly turn him into a responsible adult.

Another benefit of giving a child increasing amounts of responsibility is that it gives him a way of finding out what he's made of, who he is. By learning to do things for himself, to pay for his own mistakes, to rely on himself, he learns what he can expect from himself, and can make an accurate assessment of his own potential.

Perhaps the toughest trick to proper observance of the principle of responsibility is fulfilling our responsibility to ourselves and to society, while at the same time not interfering with the child's sense of responsibility. How can the parent be *himself* without interfering with the child's right to be *himself*? Take, for example, the problem of school work. How can parents facilitate their child's learning without taking over for him? Each parent is responsible for encouraging his child to learn, and has the right to fulfill this responsibility by setting rewards and punishments, as long as he respects the child's right to choose either to do the work or to accept the consequences. Wade's father approached the problem by telling him that he couldn't watch TV until he had done his homework and had done it acceptably. But he reiterated that it was still up to him to choose whether he'd do the homework or do without TV. The first night, Wade turned on the TV without having done his homework. Fortunately, Wade's dad had learned not to react, but to let the consequences speak for themselves. In the old days, his response could have been picked up on the Richter scale; and Wade would have been more irritated than a centipede with corns. Dad now realized, however, that this kind of reaction was positively reinforcing to Wade, because it was a means of manipulating his father's feelings. Now, Mr. Brock simply empathized, and invoked the rule: "I know you'd really like to watch television, and I'm sorry you can't because you haven't done your homework." Soon Wade plopped himself in front of the TV again, and announced that his homework was done. "Let me see your assignments," requested Mr. Brock. Wade's work came about as close to its objective as the Tower of Babel. In the past, Mr. Brock would have lectured, "Now you have to do it over again. It's twice as much work when you do it wrong and have to re-do it." In the past, keeping after Wade in this manner had turned Dad into something resembling a keystone cop; now, he was Mr. Cool. He simply said, "Your homework is not done acceptably," and handed the paper back. He did not even add the statement, "So you can't watch television." Wade eventually caught on: no homework, no TV. But, he seemed to be willing to give up his viewing rather than do the work. This, of course, meant that the TV consequence was not strong enough or possibly ill-suited to Wade's unique reinforcement preferences. In response, Mr. Brock simply upped the stakes (in this case, no homework, no allowance).

For my final illustration of the principle of responsibility, I'll take a couple of extreme examples from another helping situation which is similar in many ways to that of the parent and child: the therapist-client relationship. Carl Rogers, the author of *On Becoming a Person* and the marriage text, *Becoming Partners*, in commenting on responsibility in psychotherapy, states:

But is the therapist willing to give the client full freedom as to outcomes? Is he genuinely willing for the client to organize and direct his life? Is he willing for him to choose goals that are social or antisocial, moral or immoral? If not, it seems doubtful that therapy will be a profound experience for the client. Even more difficult, is he willing for the client to choose regression rather than growth or maturity? To choose neuroticism rather than mental health? Or to choose to reject help rather than to accept it? To choose death rather than life? To me it appears that only as the therapist is completely willing that *any* outcomes, *any* direction, may be chosen—only then does he realize the vital strength of the capacity and potentiality of the individual for constructive action. It is as he is willing for death to be the choice, that life is chosen; for neuroticism to be the choice, that a healthy normality is chosen.

Explicit in these words is the idea that responsibility for even life itself should not be taken away. Most people would not be able to restrain themselves from physically intervening if they could prevent someone from committing suicide; nonetheless, Rogers' point may be a valid one. His views were certainly vindicated in the experience of one of my colleagues. One afternoon, his phone rang. On the other end of the line was one of his patients, a young woman of twenty. She was phoning from the fourteenth floor of a hotel, and identified her room by number. She went on to say that she was at that moment sitting in the window, and was planning to jump. A naive or unskilled helper might have responded with pleas for her not to jump and with other forms of persuasion or logic. This therapist relied solely on the techniques of responsibility. He began to empathize with her, trying to understand her feelings of hopelessness and depression. After a few minutes, she began to talk more freely. Before either of them realized it, the conversation had lasted for thirty minutes and the patient agreed to meet the next day to discuss the matter further. Upon appearing for her appointment, she confirmed that she had honestly intended to jump. Her fantasy was that when she called her therapist, he would write a note to his secretary while keeping the patient on the line. The secretary would call the hotel and relay the information to the house detective. He would then burst through the locked door in an attempt to grab her before she jumped. She went on to say that when this happened, it would be her cue to jump. The therapist was the only person in her life who had granted her complete freedom of responsibility. In a time of depression, this was the only thing that gave her any desire to live. She had, therefore, decided to conduct an ultimate test of his confidence in her. She had decided to test his willingness to grant her responsibility by seeing if he would give her the right to either live or die. When the therapist, because of his firm belief in the principle of responsibility, did not take over for the patient, he passed this most crucial test. Thus, refusing to take over for someone else is an effective way to love and value. Giving responsibility can be dangerous, but so can taking it away. Love which attempts to manipulate, even if the manipulation is felt to be for the other person's own good, is a lesser form of love.

Appendix

If you have read the main body of this book closely, if you have studied the twenty principles carefully, reviewed them thoroughly, discussed them with your spouse, if you are as familiar with those principles as you are with the faces of your own children, and if you apply those principles conscientiously every minute of every day and twice as often on weekends, YOU WILL *STILL* HAVE PROBLEMS.

If you don't want problems then don't have children, don't go into business for yourself, don't take up farming, don't even get up in the morning. A coma or a catatonic stupor may be your only refuge from problems. Certainly no one has come up with a sure-fire way of rearing children without having problems. You may even be tempted to name your children Excedrin Headache Number One and Excedrin Headache Number Two instead of John and Mary. But if you understand the principles I've given you and if you apply them with the best of your ability, you should at least have fewer problems and be better equipped to deal with the problems that you can't avoid. And speaking of problems you can't avoid, that's just what this appendix is all about. Each section is devoted to one specific problem, the sort that can befall even the best of parents. My purpose is to give you a little additional information about these problems and to show you how the principles you've just read about can be called upon for help. But even if you aren't faced with these particular problems, reading this appendix should give you a better grasp of how to use the principles in coping with the problems that *do* come your way.

1

Rule Making

If you've decided to take responsibility for childrearing—to be in charge of your family—then you will inevitably want some household rules.

No swinging from the chandeliers.

The cat must not be set on fire *in the house*.

Close the refrigerator door. But not with your sister inside.

I can't tell you *what* rules you should have. That's a matter of personal values and lifestyle. Some people cherish privacy above all else, so they have rules to protect themselves from intrusions. Others like it quiet, so their rules govern decibel level. And kids differ: some families have to have rules that require a minimum number of hours spent in studying; others have to set limits on the amount of time spent in bookish activity to insure that Junior's legs don't atrophy from lack of use. So I can't tell you what rules you should have, but I can give you some thoughts on setting up good rules.

Whenever possible, parents should discuss all rules between themselves and reach agreement on a rule *before* announcing it to the children. Nothing is more likely to create havoc than to have one parent encouraging an activity that the other parent abhors:

Father: Sure, you can climb the trees. Do you good. Build up your muscles, give you confidence. Besides, it's fun.

Mother: Get down from that tree before you break your stupid neck. Are you *crazy* or something?

It won't take the kids long to figure out where the inconsistencies lie, and then they've got you by the ears.

As the children get older, it's a good idea to discuss the rules with the kids, too. Even four-year-olds can offer intelligent contributions to a discussion of rules.

One advantage of discussing the rules and explaining them to the child is that the rules will usually end up being clear and unambiguous. A vague rule can be worse than no rule at all:

Mom: George, we've decided that we need a rule about your table manners.

George: What's wrong with my table manners?

Mom: Well, for one thing, we think you should use a knife and fork.

George: The Chinese eat with their fingers. I've seen them on TV.

Mom: Fine. But until you buy your ticket to China or make other arrangements, you'll have to eat as we do if you eat at this house.

A clearly stated rule makes enforcement easier and reduces violations. For instance, a rule might be set that says that a child must play in her own back yard unless she has permission to leave. There is, obviously, no great danger if the child steps one foot over the boundary line, but the line must be drawn somewhere. If one foot is OK, then what about two feet over? Two yards over? Two hundred yards? It is better to be accused of arbitrariness than to set indefinite limits for a child.

Next, parents should be sure they are right before setting up a rule. If they discuss the rules between themselves, the flaws will usually show themselves. And bad rules can be particularly disruptive. If a rule is unfair, for example, the child will rightfully—and possibly righteously—object. That will put you in an awkward position.

Another reason for being sure you are right is that if one or both parents are unsure of the rule's value, they will hesitate to enforce it, and kids generally are faster than a speeding bullet to pick up on such hesitation, and they will try to discourage your enforcement.

And what do you do if you make a rule and then decide it was a mistake? Change it. But be particularly careful that the new rule is one you can live with. Otherwise you get a reputation as a fickle leader: one minute the rule is "don't do this," then it's "do it or else."

All rules and changes in rules should be announced before you begin enforcing them. Remember, children rightfully resent being surprised by punishment for an act previously disregarded.

Don: Whaddaya mean I can't go to the picnic?

Dad: That's your punishment for putting chewing gum on the table legs.

Don: But I *always* put my chewing gum on the table legs.

Dad: Not any more you don't. We're tired of that business and we've decided you're too old for that kind of thing. And besides, this last wad wasn't even sugarless.

Even Don deserves protection against ex-post-facto laws. It's better to announce the rules and *then* enforce them. If you get caught without an important rule, say you're making it now and it will apply to the next offense, but no punishment this time around.

It will help matters a lot if you will make it a point to keep the rules to a minimum. If you start listing all the behaviors you expect your children (or any other human beings for that matter) to abide by, it may turn out to be several light years long. You expect the check-out clerk in the grocery store to bag your groceries, you expect him to put the ice cream in the refrigerator bag, the meats and eggs on top, the canned goods on the bottom. You expect your bus driver to stop at the curb, not in the middle of the street. And on and on. There are millions of things that we expect other people to do, and millions of other things that we expect them to refrain from doing. We have laws to identify only a fraction of those, and even with the hundreds of laws on the books, they don't begin to cover all the behaviors that could be governed by rules.

The same is true in your family. You can't possibly have a comprehensive list of do's and don'ts. Most family rules cover duties or areas which are a habitual problem or involve safety:

"You can ride your bicycle as far as State Street, but no further."

"These are medicines, not candy, and they are dangerous. Stay away from them."

"You're flunking out of college. If you can't maintain a passing average, you'll have to find someone else to subsidize you."

Keeping the rules to a minimum will also prevent your family life from turning into a game of cops and robbers, with the parents devoted enforcers and the kids the villains who must be forever on their toes to escape detection from the familial fuzz.

Finally, parents must commit themselves to following through with the rules. There is no "now and then" about rules. Parents must enforce the limits they have prescribed. And enforcement will be easier if they make up their minds that there will be NO exceptions. If it's a good rule, why should it sometimes be suspended? And if it should be suspended now and then, then maybe it's not a good rule.

The trouble with looking the other way, with saying "OK, just this once," is that it ruins the clarity of a rule. You said not to leave the yard without permission, but last week Richard left and you overlooked it. If it was OK to leave without permission then, why not now? You open up a hornet's nest when you succumb to the temptation to look the other way.

And if you don't always follow through on a rule, then you have taught the child that rules are made to be broken. To the child, every rule should be tested in order to see whether it is enforced or not. And if a violation is punished today, then try again tomorrow, when Mom's in a better mood. Say what you will, your behavior will make the greatest impression. You may say that one exception doesn't mean anything, but to the child, it does.

Being 100% consistent is a challenge for anyone, but more difficult for some parents than others. Some will feel that their particular personalities make them too impulsive always to respond with such carefully considered responses. They are likely to spank first and think later; or just give in to the child rather than be consistent, because giving in is easier. Now, all of us recognize that some individuals are more impulsive than others. Some people have more self control than the valedictorian dog in an obedience school, while others shoot from the hip. So what does a parent do when he finds himself in the latter category? Fortunately, or unfortunately, there is only one answer. He does *whatever* is necessary to curb his impulsivity and allow himself to be 100% consistent. It will be easier for some of us than others, but the standard is the same for all. No one should be granted permission to be ineffective as a parent because of any trait or weakness in character. Too much is at stake for parents, for the child, for society. And after all, parenthood is not the only place where individuals are told to grit their teeth, to bear down, and to do whatever is necessary to get the job done. No coach in his half-time speech ever tells the players who are tired to take it easy the second half. No lieutenant has ever yelled, "Let the courageous charge and the cowards retreat!" Or, "Those with fighting instincts press on, those with reservations take five." In competition and combat, everyone is told to do his best. If his best is not good enough, he is told to change it so that it *is* good enough. The standards are never lowered to suit the traits of those in the struggle. To lower standards for impulsive or otherwise handicapped parents would be to "cop out."

The task confronting one single parent of my acquaintance proved especially difficult, but rather than "cop out," she did what had to be done. This divorced mother sought consultation because her teenaged daughter refused to obey rules. For one thing, she persisted in entertaining boyfriends in the home while her mother was at work. The mother was concerned that one boy was smoking marijuana and was afraid he might get her and her daughter in trouble with the law. Whenever the mother tried to enforce the rules, an argument would break out and the daughter would threaten to run away. The mother would make whatever concessions were necessary, fearing that the daughter might slip into a hippie-like existence.

When the mother sought help, she was encouraged to set whatever rules she felt appropriate, then to enforce them consistently. If the daughter felt that she could not tolerate these rules, she was free to make other living arrangements through her father, a foster home, or a state institution. As soon as the mother enacted the new policy, the daughter stopped threatening to run away. Nevertheless, she was slow in complying with the *other* rules (not writing on the walls, not having a boyfriend in the house when the mother was away, and so forth). At my suggestion, she told her daughter that she was unwilling to provide a house to be defaced or used to entertain boyfriends in a manner she could not accept. For this reason, the daughter was given a choice: She must repair any damage she had done within twenty-four hours, and not have boys over during the mother's working hours. If she refused she would be referred to the local children's court as a "child in need of supervision." After two weeks of acceptable behavior, the daughter called the mother's bluff. She adorned her bedroom and one hallway with psychedelic designs made from nonwashable paint. This was done by her and a boyfriend during the mother's working hours.

Although it was quite painful for the mother, she contacted the children's court, where she and her daughter were referred to a counselor. But when the time came for them to go, the daughter refused. The children's court was called, and a police car was sent to pick them up. The daughter remained quite subdued during the ensuing talk with the counselor. She was told that she was not, at this time, being brought to trial, but that a recurrence of the same circumstances would bring her before a judge. If that happened, she would undoubtedly be judged a child in need of supervision and be placed in either a foster home, an orphanage, a home for the emotionally disturbed, or a correctional institution. The daughter was quite surprised that her mother had allowed her to become involved with the court. She ceased testing her mother from this point on and complied with the basic regulations of the home.

One problem that every parent has is deciding what to do about rules—what they should be, how they should be enforced, how much say the child should have in deciding them, and so forth. If you'll spend some time thinking about the points I've made about rules *before* you make them, you may save yourself some aches and pains later on.

2

Sex Education

Sex Is Only A Three Letter Word, So How Can It Be Bad?

The first thing to understand about sex education is that you do not get to choose whether there will be any. That is a foregone conclusion. If a child lives in a community, if he interacts with other people, he will receive sex education. The only questions concern *what* your child will be taught about sex, *when*, and *by whom*. If parents wait too long to discuss such topics, the child will be taught by peers whose lectures may sound as if they were written by the Happy Hooker.

Some parents wish desperately that this were not the case. They like to believe that sex is like calculus, a sophisticated subject that no one thinks about until they have to. These parents often think that "one day" they will have a "man-to-man" or "woman-to-woman" talk with their child—when the child is ready. Trouble is, their children are never ready, and tomorrow is always soon enough. But, assuming that parents want to be the first to instruct their children, it will be necessary to start early. Otherwise, our instructions may go the same route as the father's sex training in the jingle:

He took me to the parlor
And quietly closed the door.
Then told me about some things
I'd heard five years before.

Tomorrow is *not* soon enough, and sex is not calculus. If you want your child to have the best sex education you can provide, begin today. With or without a parent's cooperation, with or without a parent's permission, sex education begins early. Even the new-born baby is treated differently if it is a boy than if it is a girl. He is held differently, played with differently. From these interactions, the child develops a sense of sexual identity—the notion that one is male or female—and researchers believe that a child's sexual identity may be formed well before he is able to understand such things, perhaps as early as eighteen months, or even younger.

So even in infancy a child is learning about sex in a general way. Of course, the two-year-old does not understand about intercourse, orgasm, and impotence, but he does see that people express affection for one another physically, and he begins to notice that males and females are particularly fond of showing such affection for each other. Long before he goes off to school, the child knows that men and women tend to live together in pairs, and that these unions often involve children, though he may not be sure where the children come from.

It is also important to establish intimacy between parent and child during the earliest years so that sexual topics can be discussed comfortably. A college-level lecture on the anatomy, physiology, and psychology of sex will mean little to a five-year-old. This is illustrated by the story of six-year-old Leona who came home from school one day and asked, "Mom, where did I come from?" Mom braced herself against the question she had long dreaded and began a well-memorized lecture on sperms and eggs and intercourse and fetuses and vaginas and birth. Thirty minutes later, the mother, feeling frayed but rather proud of herself, asked Leona if she had any questions. "No," Leona said. "Sally says she came from Ohio, and I was just wondering where I came from."

The moral of the story is to try to match your answer to the child's ability to understand. This does not mean making up facts: you did not get your baby at the baby factory, nor did you buy him at a store or find him on your doorstep or get him from a stork. These are lies, and parents more often tell them to relieve their own embarrassment about sexual matters than because the child is too young to understand. Tell the truth, but keep the sophistication and details of your answer at a level the child can understand.

In the preschool years children should be taught the names of various body parts. Their *real* names, not ridiculous euphemisms. A penis is a penis, not a weenie or a Thing. A vagina is a vagina, even in a three-year-old girl, though you may find that hard to believe. Many parents seem to believe that their children do not have penises and vaginas until they are eighteen, at which time, no doubt in the dark of night, these organs presumably metamorphose from wee-wees and pee-pee holes into penises and vaginas. It doesn't happen that way, and the parent who uses euphemisms to refer to sexual organs will find it difficult to talk about sex later on: you cannot talk matter-of-factly about sex after you have spent ten or fifteen years using terms that suggest sex is so terrible one cannot even speak about it except in a disguised language.

Generally, when a child *asks* about a sexual matter, it's time to talk about it. But it's also a good idea for the parent to bring up topics if the child seems old enough to understand. Pregnancy, for example, can be explained in an elementary fashion before the child begins first grade. The explanation should include the fact that the baby is conceived and develops in the mother's uterus. But the uterus is not a stomach, so don't call it a stomach. You might define uterus as a cavity or space near the stomach.

Children usually wonder how babies are made by about age six. For helpful suggestions on how to answer this question, I suggest that you read the article by Dr. Anne Bernstein in the January, 1976 issue of *Psychology Today*. Your explanation should include the fact that a sperm from the father combines with an egg inside the mother and that this grows inside the mother's uterus into a baby.

The next question is, "How does the father's sperm get inside the mother's body to meet up with her egg?'' Your answer should explain that the father puts his penis into the mother's vagina and that sperm comes out of the penis into the mother. This may be a good time to point out that this is known as intercourse.

A child of five or six may not completely understand your explanation, but that's no problem: he'll come back for more information when he needs to. The important thing is that you discuss this and other sexual topics matter-of-factly; if you do, your child will come back when he wants clarification.

Note the deferential manner in which a potentially touchy topic is handled in the ensuing examples:

Michele: (age six) Teri is going to get a little brother.

Mother: (trying to avoid the topic) That's nice.

Michele: Isn't that neat?

Mother: (nervously) I guess, now run along.

As you can see, Michele's mother passed that opportunity by as though it were a hitchiker in handcuffs. But unfortunately, sex education *did* take place. Michele was told indirectly that human reproduction is either too boring, or possibly too scary, to be discussed. To make matters worse, mother missed a 24-carat opportunity to cultivate intimacy. There was a better way to handle it:

Michele: Teri is going to get a little brother.

Mother: How about that, so Teri's mother is pregnant and they want a little boy.

Michele: Yes, and they're going to get one, because that's what they ordered.

Mother: Well, you know that parents can't order a boy or a girl; they can *want* whatever they wish, but they have to wait until the baby is born to see what they get.

Michele: Well, I thought that's the way it was, but Teri said it worked differently.

Mother: Well, you were right.

Michele: Remember when you said babies come from the mother's tummy?

Mother: Not exactly the tummy; it's from the uterus which is here (takes Michele's hand and puts it over her lower abdomen) just below the tummy.

Michele: I remember you said that there was a seed in the tummy which made a baby grow, and that the seed came from the father.

Mother: (not bothering to correct the daughter a second time about tummy vs. uterus) That's right.

Michele: But how does the seed from the father get into the mother's tummy?

Mother: (clears her throat nervously; well, no parent is perfect) It comes out of the father through his penis. He places his penis in the mother's vagina; and the seed comes out of his penis through the vagina into the place where the baby grows.

Michele: Yeah, now I remember. You told me that before, but I forgot how the last part worked.

To me there is a certain beauty in the fact that Michele forgot the mechanics of intercourse. A topic as potentially loaded and frightening as sex had obviously been discussed in such a natural way that it failed to make a lasting impression on the child. Had the mother forgotten that earlier episode, she probably would have had amnesia. But daughter's forgetting meant that the topic had simply been "defused" by the natural manner in which it was handled.

During the elementary school years, from ages six to twelve, parents should try to foster a sense of sexual identity—masculinity or feminity—without insisting on rigid adherence to traditional sex roles. Comments such as "Boys don't cry," are not obviously untrue (boys *do* cry; so do men) but they make the child feel that he is not what he should be; he is supposed to be a boy, but since he is crying, he must be a girl. Similarly, girls should not be told they can't do things that boys can do (they can and they should).

As the child progresses through the elementary grades, parents should talk more extensively about sexual anatomy. Both boys and girls should be told about the existence of breasts, ovaries, testes, and the function of these organs. During this period there should be discussions about morals and how sex and morals are related.

No one can tell you what your morals should be, but I can tell you that severe negative views about sex tend to be more common in people with poor sexual adjustment and emotional problems. It is a thoroughly proven fact that masturbation, sexual fantasies and exploring one's own body are normal events in the lives of nearly all children. Trying to suppress such activities will only make the child feel that he or she is some sort of freak, when the fact is that everybody else is doing the same thing.

I am not saying that you have to be an ardent advocate of free love and open marriage to produce a healthy child. But telling a child that masturbating, exploring his or her body, or experimenting with sex will make him deaf and blind, make his brain rot or his teeth fall out, will instill guilt and fear of sex and everything connected with it. You cannot spend twenty years of your life learning to think of sex as dirty, frightening, and sinful and then suddenly in adulthood accept sex as a natural part of life.

In the latter part of the elementary grade years, children should be told about the changes they can expect in adolescence. Girls particularly are in for a terrifying shock if they are not prepared for their first menstruation. Again, such matters should be dealt with honestly: menstruation is not a sickness, nor is it "the curse"; it is a natural physiological process that is part of growing up.

There's more to puberty than menstruation, and girls should be told about the changes that will take place: increased hip size, enlargement of breasts, the growth of pubic hair. Boys should be told that their voices will change, they will begin to grow beards, pubic hair will appear, and that they may have nocturnal emissions (wet dreams).

All of these changes are normal, and except in the case of disease or malfunctioning hormonal systems, they happen to nearly everyone. The following example illustrates how one father made the most of an opportunity to have a discussion on the topic:

Son: I don't think I'm going to go out for Little League baseball this year. I'm pretty good at football and wrestling, but I'm just not that good in baseball.

Father: Well, one thing you ought to keep in mind is that within the next year a lot of changes will take place in your body. It's called puberty. After that happens some things are different than they were before. Sometimes boys who weren't very good in sports begin to excel. Do you know the kind of changes I'm talking about?

Son: No, I don't think so.

Father: Well, you know how Stuart and Wally (older neighborhood boys) started growing so fast last year? Their voices changed and they started growing beards.

Son: Oh, yeah, now I know what you're talking about.

Father: And you've probably noticed some of your other friends are beginning to grow very fast and other changes are occurring in their bodies, like hair under their arms and around their penises.

Son: Yeah, I know about that.

Father: After these changes occur, boys are usually capable of fathering a child. I'm really trying to tell you two things. One is that you shouldn't make up your mind too early about how good you are in a sport. The other is that you can expect a lot of changes in your body and in your behavior in the next couple of years.

Son: I see.

Father: Any time you have questions or want to talk more about it, just let me know.

Son: I'd like to know everything about that kind of stuff.

Father: Then why don't you get some questions in your mind and tonight after supper we'll sit down and discuss the things you want to know about. Is it a deal?

Son: It's a deal.

Here's a matter-of-fact conversation on menstruation between a father and three children, including an eleven-year-old daughter. The youngest participant is Arthur, age eight, and the eldest is Mark, age fifteen. At the time of this discussion, the family was on its way to church:

Mark: Why did Mom have us stop at the drug store? What's she buying there?

Father: She's having her menstrual period and she ran out of tampons, so we stopped where she could buy some. (then addressing the eleven-year-old daughter) Fran, didn't you and Mom talk about the fact that she was menstruating? Do you understand what is going on?

Fran: Yes, Mom and I have talked about menstruation before and she told me that was why she wanted to stop at the store.

Father: Has Mom told you about what to expect when you begin to menstruate?

Fran: Yes.

Father: Do you feel like you've been given enough information and you are prepared for this when it happens?

Fran: I think so.

Mark: Well, I've heard about it, but I don't know very much about it.

119

Arthur: What's mensuration?

Father: *Menstruation*. Well, why don't I tell you a few things about menstruation, then you ask questions.

By the time the child leaves home, he should have learned about foreplay and orgasm (in men *and* women) and about problems such as the inability to have orgasms, premature ejaculation, and impotence. If children have a good understanding of these kinds of facts, they should be well prepared to make a good sexual adjustment in adulthood.

The following is a list of recommended resources for parents wishing to improve their level of information and skill as sex educators:

Family Planning Perspectives (available free of charge from the Center for Family Planning, 515 Madison Avenue, New York, New York 10022).

Emko Newsletter (a monthly digest of sex information free of charge from Emko Newsletter, 7912 Manchester Avenue, St. Louis, Missouri 63143).

Journal of Marriage and the Family (available from the National Council of Family Relations, 1219 University Avenue, S.E., Minneapolis, Minnesota 55414).

The following materials are primarily for the child. But I list them with an admonition to parents: under no circumstances should we feel our sex education obligations have been met if we simply give the child a book to read. Most kids will probably have already gotten everything they can from that method by peeping at *National Geographic*.

American Medical Association Series:

A Parent's Privilege (for parents of young children).

A Story About You (grades 4, 5, and 6).

Finding Yourself (junior high school).

Preparation for Marriage (16 to 20 years of age).

The Facts Aren't Enough (for adults who have the responsibility for older children).

These works are available from the American Medical Association, 535 N. Dearborn Street, Chicago, Illinois.

Recommended books:

Facts About Sex: A Basic Guide, by Sol Gordon (John Day Book Co.). ($1.90 paperback). Also, *Where Did I Come From* by Peter Mayle (Lyle Stuart, Inc.) (for elementary and junior high school-aged children).

Understanding Sex: A Young Person's Guide by Allen F. Guttmacher ($.95, Signet Books) (for teenagers).

Common Sense Sex by Ronald M. Masser (Beacon Press) (for college students).

Complete Sex Education for Parents, Teenagers, and Young Adults by James L. McCary (Van Nostrand Reinhold, 450 W. 33, New York, N.Y. 10001) (best all around book).

3

Drug Abuse

Remember when grass was something you mowed, and only martyrs got stoned?

I can remember when glue was something you used to build model airplanes and hard stuff referred to trigonometry. To me, "shooting" means making a movie, and if you've got "uppers," you've got half a set of false teeth. So much of the drug users' jargon is part of our everyday language that it may seem that the entire country spends most of its time popping or shooting or smoking or guzzling something.

But while we may hear more about drugs than our own parents used to, that doesn't mean that drug abuse is new. This is one problem that parents have had to worry about for thousands of years. You'll have to worry about it, too.

You've got several things working against you in your efforts to keep your child from becoming a dope fiend. For one thing, many drugs are popular because they're fun. Fact is: if it were not rewarding to smoke a joint, people wouldn't pay hard cash for marijuana.

And a child's curiosity (ordinarily a very healthy thing) will fight you: a child is going to want to try things for himself, to see what all the fuss is about.

Perhaps your most serious enemy will be peer group pressure. Children care a great deal about what their age mates think of their behavior. In adolescence, children come under incredible pressure to go along with the crowd, to do what "everybody" is doing. The opinions of their parents and other fuddy-duddies have little impact:

"Come on Marylou, drink the kerosene; whatsa matter, you chicken?"

Against these forces parents may seem helpless. One thing is for sure, you should not sit by until a child is sixteen and then start looking for needle punctures. Whatever you do to combat the problem of drug abuse, you'd better start early.

I think there are four fronts on which parents can fight the problem of drug abuse: personal adjustment, parental modeling of responsible drug use, developing a child's sense of responsibility, and giving the child straight information about drugs.

The most important thing to keep in mind about drug education is that drug problems are not due primarily to a lack of facts. Information is just not where it's at. The difference between drug abuse and adaptive behavior is more often a matter of personality and character development. Personality and character, of course, refer to traits such as moral values, impulse control, and feelings of adequacy. What codes of drug-related conduct is a child likely to acquire? Will he develop good impulse control? Does he or she feel adequate or will drug assistance be required for a feeling of acceptance by self and others? These are the real questions, and experiences in the home, not the classroom, are responsible for the development of these traits.

A child's character and personality may also determine what he does when we try to teach him about drugs. Unless we have done a good job of fostering intimacy, he may never ask us about drugs or even listen when we try to provide such information.

Modeling

I've already described the powerful effect that parental modeling can have on a child's behavior in chapter seven. It might be a good idea for you to go over the chapter again and think of how modeling applies specifically to drug abuse.

The parent who has a cocktail before dinner, takes a sleeping pill before retiring, and then asks what villain led his child into drug abuse will find his answer in the mirror. Many adults rely heavily on sleeping pills, alcohol, tobacco, tranquilizers and muscle relaxants. They feel tense and take a pill. They *think* they're getting a headache, so they down a couple of aspirin. They have a couple of drinks to loosen up after a hard day. They chain smoke cigarettes while waiting for an important phone call. And somehow they think that none of this has anything to do with the behavior of their children.

"After all," they defend themselves, "I'm not *advocating* that my kids use these drugs. I don't tell Molly that the pills I'm popping are tranquilizers or that drugs are a good way of dealing with stress." Or some parents say, "Well, tobacco and alcohol aren't drugs; I mean real dope." Again, your kids are probably too smart to be influenced by your misinformation about what is and isn't a drug, what is or isn't habit forming, what is or isn't a threat to health, etc.

Like it or not, you can't fool kids. They get the message: happiness is a pharmaceutical product. If you want your child to believe that drugs are not the source of happiness, then you will have to demonstrate that you believe it.

I'm not saying that parents should never take drugs. What I am saying is that your kids will tend to adopt your use of drugs: if you smoke, they will smoke; if you drink, they will drink; if you take pills to get yourself up or bring yourself down, they will too.

In short, if you behave as though drugs are an important source of pleasure, the cure for every ill, the solution to every problem, your child will probably behave the same way. And no amount of lecturing or explaining will overcome the influence of your own example.

Responsibility

A third way that parents can fight the threat of drug abuse is by applying the principle of responsibility discussed in chapter twenty. Avoiding drug abuse requires that the child make intelligent decisions. Ultimately, the child decides whether to sniff glue, snort coke, smoke pot, drink booze or shoot horse. And unless you are willing to keep your child under lock and key forever, you will not be able to prevent him from using these drugs if he chooses to do so. It is foolish for a parent to assume responsibilities that ought to be turned over to the child, and then be disappointed when the child behaves irresponsibly. It is madness to think that a child can spend one or more decades relying entirely on his parents' judgment and then suddenly make brilliant decisions on his own. Specifically, parents should make it clear to their children that decisions on drugs are purely their own, as are the benefits and consequences (fines, lawyer fees, etc.).

Drug Information

A parents' influence concerning drugs depends upon his credibility. Unfortunately, in some families drug education is the greatest threat to parents' credibility since Junior found out there really wasn't a Boogie Man. Many parents are more poorly informed, possess a greater number of biases and are less willing to allow children to decide things for themselves in this area than they are about sex. Each of these factors distracts from a parents' believability, which in turn diminishes his effectiveness as a drug educator. Parents must give their children accurate, unprejudiced information about drugs and not in a single lecture at age sixteen, but beginning early in childhood.

Drug education is a lot like sex education, and parents make many of the same mistakes. For example, some parents avoid discussing drugs. They tell the child that he's too young to understand or that he'll learn about that when he's older.

When they do discuss drugs, parents often feel obliged to give a very biased view. They figure they'll exaggerate to make their point stronger. The immediate effect of this sort of scare tactic is often what the parent wants. But the long-range effect is that the parents' credibility is eroded.

If you tell your kids that pot will rot their brains and make their sex organs shrink, they'll eventually find out you were wrong. Then when you tell them that LSD may cause horrifying hallucinations, how are they to know that this time you're giving them the straight scoop? The other kids are talking about how much fun an acid trip is. How's a person to know who's lying? One way to find out the truth is to go along with the crowd and try it.

The younger a child is, the more elementary your discussion of drugs will have to be. But age is never an excuse for making up lies. The following example illustrates how parents can talk about drugs with their children:

Mother: Kids, I had a very interesting talk with a friend of mine today. She has a fourteen-year-old son who's gotten hooked on diet pills.

Marlene: (twelve years old) What's his name? Is it anybody we know?

Mother: His name is Carl Johnson, and I don't think you know him. He goes to a different school.

Carlton: (fourteen years old) What happened to him?

Mother: He's been taking diet pills in order to lose some weight. After a while, he began to act strangely. He would sometimes blow his stack for no reason at all. Later he'd say he was sorry. He didn't know why he did such things, but he just couldn't seem to help himself. The parents finally took him to a doctor who took him off the pills. But now he can't seem to do anything without them. He is unable to study or even to practice the piano, which he used to love to do. Anyway, I just wanted to tell you kids about this because I felt you'd never know about things like this unless I brought them up.

Marlene: I'm glad you tell us things like this. Some of the things other parents do and say about drugs are really stupid.

Mother: Like what?

Marlene: Well, I know one boy whose parents caught him smoking grass in his bedroom. For punishment they told him he couldn't drive the car for one day. They thought that much punishment was a big deal.

Carlton: I know some parents who go the other way. This one girl whose parents caught her using drugs got sent away to some kind of school or camp. No one has heard from her since. She wasn't that bad off.

Mother: Where do you kids feel you've gotten your ideas about drugs?

Marlene: Part of mine are based on what you and Dad believe. And we've had some programs at school that taught me a lot. One of the best things was Drug Awareness Week. There were policemen and lawyers who told us what our rights were. Like if you're arrested, you don't have to say anything. I really appreciated that. It made me feel like they were being fair and telling us both sides, rather than just brainwashing us. But I think the main thing that turned me against drugs is talking to Letha Weeks. She told me about how taking drugs really messed her up.

Carlton: I think that is where I have gotten most of my beliefs about drugs— from people I know who take them.

Mother: How do you mean?

Carlton: Well, all the kids I know who take drugs are really messed up. I just don't want to be like them. I'd rather be like the kids who don't take drugs.

Mother: That makes a lot of sense.

Carlton: And I think I've gotten some of my beliefs from what you've said.

Mother: Like what?

124

Carlton:	Things you told me about smoking, drinking, and drugs like heroin and LSD. I didn't know they could cause diseases and how you can get addicted to them.
Mother:	That's very interesting.
Carlton:	I think the most important thing that you told me about drugs was that it was up to me whether or not I used them. But you also said I couldn't be allowed to use them in the house. At first I thought it was pretty dumb when you said that went for smoking, too. Then I found out there are separate sections in airplanes for smokers and non-smokers.
Mother:	Does that help it make more sense?
Carlton:	Well, I'm not going to smoke. But if I did, I think I should be allowed to do it in my room.

Parents will find giving their children straight facts about drugs a lot easier if they know the facts themselves. Unfortunately, parents often try to provide information they themselves do not have. Here are a few facts about some of the most commonly abused drugs:

Nicotine and alcohol are probably the most dangerous drugs in use in this country today. I base this statement on the fact that these two drugs are the most widely used, and both are known to cause serious health problems.

A majority of Americans smoke, despite the evidence that smoking is related to cancer, heart trouble, emphysema and other diseases. The chances of getting lung cancer, for instance, are eight times greater for a smoker than a non-smoker.

There are approximately one hundred million Americans who drink and eight to ten percent of them are "problem drinkers." We wouldn't ride in an airplane that had a one in ten chance of crashing, yet more people survive plane crashes than alcoholism. Alcohol is a toxin that kills brain tissue and damages the heart. A liver damaged by alcohol is harder to put together again than Humpty Dumpty, and half of all highway deaths involve someone who has been drinking. The old standbys, booze and tobacco, are by far the greatest threats of the readily available drugs.

Marijuana does distort perception of distances and time, and these effects would certainly make driving hazardous. Marijuana is also known to adversely effect achievement, motivation and objective perception of self and one's own achievements. Links between marijuana and some birth defects have also been established. However, marijuana is apparently not as addictive or habit forming, as are both tobacco and alcohol.

Many of the other consciousness-altering drugs have even less to recommend them. LSD, for instance, may cause birth defects in the user's offspring. And there have been numerous reports of flashbacks—bad trips that happen long after the drug is taken.

Inhalants are among the most hazardous of the hallucinogens. Glue and aerosol sprays can damage lungs, the nervous system and the kidneys. They can cause mental retardation and even death.

Stimulants or "uppers" are bad news. They give a burst of energy that can be pleasant, but this is typically followed by depression. And people have been known to commit very bizarre and violent acts while tripping on some uppers, notably methedrine (speed).

Hard narcotics such as morphine and heroin are primarily dangerous because of the hazards in getting these illegal drugs, and because they are often injected, which makes the user susceptible to hepatitis. Heroin users also suffer from malnutrition which makes them susceptible to other diseases.

Obviously, there's a great deal more to know about drugs than I've covered here. I don't ask you to become a pharmacologist, but I do ask you to help your child get solid information about drugs. Toward that end, you may find the bibliography at the end of this chapter helpful.

One more thing. Your child makes the ultimate decision about drugs, but you get to decide whether you will support his drug habits. If you suspect that Harold is on the sauce or has taken up smoking, there is nothing in the rules that says you have to pay for his drugs. You can withhold an allowance if you think it will be spent on Coors, Camels or Cactus (peyote).

If you provide a good model for your child concerning the use of drugs, if you help him learn to accept responsibilities, and if you give him accurate information about drugs, the chances are very good that your child will avoid becoming a lush, a chain smoker, or a wide-eyed dope fiend.

Parents wishing to know more about the effects of drug abuse, or wanting to learn how to spot the signs that a child is taking drugs, are encouraged to contact their local school systems, juvenile courts or state and county health departments. The U.S. Department of Health, Education and Welfare also has excellent information. The reading material listed below is especially recommended:

Drug Abuse: The Chemical Cop-Out (available from Blue Cross/Blue Shield).
Recent Research on Narcotics, LSD, Marijuana and Other Dangerous Drugs (available from the National Institute of Mental Health, Washington, D.C.).
Before Your Kid Tries Drugs—This work includes a glossary of terms and a bibliography of other works including films (available from National Institute of Mental Health, Washington, D.C.).
The Drug Scene by Walter May, University of California (available from Prentice-Hall, Inc., Englewood Cliffs, NJ).
Teachers and sophisticated parents may benefit from the following works:
Drug Abuse: Escape to Nowhere (available from the National Association of Health, Physical Education and Recreation, Washington, D.C.).
President's Commission on Law Enforcement, Task Force Report on Narcotics & Drug Abuse (available from the Superintendent of Documents, U.S. Government Printing Office, Washington, D.C.).

4

Moral and Religious Training

Children differ greatly in their moral and religious development. Some are miniature replicas of Billy Graham and others would turn their own parents over to a motorcycle gang in return for an autographed picture of The Boston Strangler. One reason for these differences is the type of moral education children receive. As in sex education, there is no such thing as *no* moral and religious training. The only questions concern *what* will be taught and *how*.

Tackling the job of moral and religious education really ties some parents in knots. Even parents who manage pretty well with topics such as sex and drugs can feel clumsy when it comes to handling basic questions about right and wrong and where God lives.

"It's the kind of thing that makes us wish we had stopped at having poodles," said one married graduate student. This young parent was wondering if he should send his child to church. Neither he nor his wife attended, but they felt they did not know how to provide religious training.

Some parents minimize their role as moral and spiritual educators because they feel their influence will be small compared with that of peers and teachers. Other parents abdicate responsibility for such training by saying, "I think every child should be able to make up his or her own mind about such matters."

Some parents feel that morality and religion are areas where there are no pat answers, and if it pertains to something they can only speculate about (some call that faith), it can't matter much. But morality and religion are important parts of our society; no one can simply ignore them.

One of the real tragedies of contemporary childrearing in America is that so little attention has been paid to the development of morality and religion in children. Many churches try to create the same ideas and commitments in five-year-olds as they do in fifteen-year-olds. The result is that young children are exposed to complex and confusing ideas, while adolescents and adults have their religious and moral development prematurely arrested.

The more a parent understands about human development, the better equipped he is as a religious educator. He will appreciate, for instance, that the preschool child tends to be concrete in his thinking. If a child is from a Christian home, he is likely to perceive Jesus as some kind of superman who could swim the widest lake and ascend or descend like a helicopter. The child may remain oblivious to other traits such as self-denial and compassion for the less fortunate.

Parents who understand moral development will realize that it is perfectly natural for adolescents to have religious doubts. They will also appreciate that adolescents who genuinely question their religious teachings are better off for having done so. Adolescents who feel it is a sin to question or doubt, and who never develop their *own* set of moral and religious beliefs, are less able to withstand the tests that life will bring their way.

All individuals must decide for themselves what is right and wrong. The parents' beliefs may require them to punish certain acts in order to feel that they are acting responsibly. Children, however, must decide for themselves what they believe is right and wrong. Both parent and child should understand that when the child is on his own he will be free to disregard the parents' rules.

Parents should be open and frank about their own beliefs. But the child also needs to know about views such as atheism and Buddhism which may differ from those of his parents. And these belief systems should be presented in a fair, unbiased manner. If parents are really sincere in their beliefs, they will not be afraid to expose their children to other views. Many theological seminaries do this in the training of ministers. For example, the training of a conservative Christian minister would include exposure to liberal Christianity, agnosticism, atheism, Buddhism, and existentialism. In this way he is informed about the other side, and is better able to debate on those views. Secure parents, like genuinely secure professors, will not be afraid to teach their proteges about viewpoints different from their own.

For parents who foster responsibility, there is the danger that the child may develop a set of values that differs from theirs. There is also, however, the possibility that if the child turns out different from his parents, he may turn out *better*. After all, each of us has values which are different from those of our parents, and we probably feel that our values constitute an improvement. Why then should we feel that our children's values will be worse than ours if they differ? Sören Kierkegaard, the Danish theologian of two centuries ago, said, "To impose your religious values on someone else without allowing them their own, may rob that person of his relationship with God." One comment I hear frequently from women of thirty-five to forty goes something like this: "I always felt like other people had something that I didn't have, and now I think I know what it is. They have their 'own' values." What these women are saying, of course, is that they have recognized the difference between themselves and people who acted on the basis of directly experienced rather than introjected values.

Unfortunately, some well-meaning parents take the approach that a child's values are so important that they want to *guarantee* that he will believe certain things. If, however, a child's values are to exert strong influence on his behavior, they must be based on his own experiences, not the experience of others. Otherwise, he will only give them lip service rather than really live by them. Let me illustrate how the issue of values should *not* be handled. Mrs. Franklin has just heard from a neighbor that her twelve-year-old son Ronald has told a dirty joke to some of the girls on the block.

Mrs. Franklin: Ronald, come here, I need to talk to you.

Ronald: What is it, Mom?

Mrs. Franklin: I'm just crushed. Mrs. Hertz told me a dirty joke that she says you told to Mary and Virginia.

Ronald: (looks down, says nothing)

Mrs. Franklin: It horrifies me to think of you talking that way. Just think of it, my own child is probably the type that writes those terrible things on bathroom walls. What would Reverend Cochran say? You'd better get down on your knees and ask God to forgive you. And when you're through, come in the bathroom and I'll wash your mouth out with soap.

An approach more consistent with the principle of responsibility would go like this:

Mrs. Franklin: Mrs. Hertz called today and said she thought I would like to know that you told Mary and Virginia a dirty joke.

Ronald: (still says nothing)

Mrs. Franklin: You know it's up to you to decide what kind of language to use. I just thought I should tell you about Mrs. Hertz's call.

Probably the most frequently asked question about religious education is, "Should a child be forced to go to church?" The first step in resolving this issue is for parents to ask themselves if church attendance is something they must demand in order to feel they are acting responsibly. If their answer is yes, then they should require church attendance. Otherwise the decision should be left to the child.

In most church-going families, attendance is a way of life which will not be seriously challenged until the child reaches adolescence. At that point most parents allow their children to decide for themselves whether or not they will attend.

Finally, parental modeling is the most important aspect of moral and religious education. As I've said before, children pay a great deal more attention to what we *do* than to the fine abstract lectures we give on the Golden Rule, the superiority of spiritual wealth to material wealth, the importance of church attendance, and the inherent rewards of virtue. The parent who backs into an unoccupied car in a parking lot and then sneaks off, gives a powerful lecture on his own version of the Golden Rule. The parent who brags about cheating on his income tax or about how he duped someone into buying bad merchandise has demonstrated how much he really believes in spiritual wealth. The parent who has to be dragged to religious services shows how valuable church attendance is. The parent who dodges jury duty has shown what he thinks about the intrinsic rewards of virtue.

Possibly the most vital point in all moral education is the importance of the parents themselves being committed to something. An uncommitted parent is like an unconsummated marriage. He is sterile, not because he tried and failed,

129

but because he never tried at all. He cannot provide any heuristic impact. That is, he never raises any questions in his child's mind which must be resolved. Successful resolution of moral and religious conflict can be more important to character and personality development than a brush with death. I remember one young person with unresolved existential questions who told me his parents were so uncommitted that they even took an agnostic position about agnosticism. "We never had any discussions about religion in our home," he said. "My existence has been so uneventful, that I figure if I had a near accident, *someone else's* entire life would have to flash before my eyes."

The best approach for parents is to be clear about their commitments, and free to act them out daily in the presence of their children. At the same time their behavior should not communicate to the child that he must do as the parents say or even as they do. We must develop the balance between being true to our commitments while at the same time not interfering with the right of our child to do the same thing.

There is no way around it: if you would have your child adhere to certain moral and religious beliefs, you must do so yourself. If you think you can accomplish the same thing by giving fine lectures, sending the child to religious schools or enrolling him in the Scouts, you're only fooling yourself. There is no better predictor of the religious and moral character of a person than the religious and moral behavior of his parents.

5

The Single Parent

There is nothing magical about the number two, but in general a parent who tries to rear children alone is in for trouble. The single parent has to be on duty twenty-four hours a day except when baby sitters are called. The single parent usually has to work, and that means leaving the child in a substitute's care for eight or more hours a day, and the substitute may or may not enforce the same rules you establish, may or may not reward behaviors as you would like, may or may not give the child the care you want him to have. And the single parent with two or more children may be hassled by sibling rivalry as each child competes for limited parental attention. In general, I'm not a big fan of single parenthood if it can be avoided.

But the fact is that more and more people are taking on the responsibilities of childrearing alone. Divorce is increasing, single people now adopt children, and unwed mothers keep their children rather than put them up for adoption. Parents can also find themselves alone if a spouse's work takes him away for extended periods. And sometimes death leaves a parent in sole charge of childrearing. However a parent happens to find himself alone with the duties of childrearing, I hope the hints in this chapter will make the job easier.

If you're a single parent, the first thing I suggest is that you re-read chapter one of the main body of the book, ''Who's in Charge Here.'' Whether your life will be miserable or happy will depend in large measure on the extent to which you are the head of the household. If you don't make up your mind to be in charge, you have my sympathy. The single parent who is not in control, particularly if there are two or more children, will feel like a cat at a dog show.

Once you've decided that the adult should bring up the child, and not vice versa, you're ready to consider the special problems you're apt to face. For example, as a single parent, you provide only one sex role model. It's a good idea for growing children to be in the company of adults of both sexes. This is especially important when the child is not the same sex as the parent. And very early exposure to same sex models seems to be more important than later exposure; the child who has appropriate adult models for the first four years is probably better off than the child who has those models at ages ten to fourteen. Good role models can be friends, relatives, Little League coaches, YMCA and YWCA teachers, scout leaders. It's more important to have a few models around frequently than to have several around infrequently.

Another issue you need to deal with before it becomes a problem is dating. Not the child's love life, but *yours*. You have to recognize the fact that some of your dates will be a lot less interested in your child than they are in you. This can lead to trouble, especially if the romance gets serious. The child is apt to feel that he's been abandoned, that you've found someone you prefer to him. You may get a sudden burst of discipline problems—tantrums, irritability, fighting, poor school work. I'm not sure anybody can tell you a sure-fire way to avoid this problem, but a good rule to follow is "Love me, love my child."

Make it clear to your prospective mates that you are a parent and that the two of you can't pretend that the child isn't there. If the man or woman of your life accepts this view and shows interest in the child as well as his parent, the problems should be less severe. If the boyfriend or girlfriend just can't seem to buy this view, you're headed for trouble. Sooner or later you will probably have to choose between the child and the new mate.

Single parents usually have a tougher time of it financially than couples. They are more likely to have to depend on friends or relatives for support, and this causes two problems: it adds to the stress of childrearing to know that you're hanging on by the fingertips, and it means you have less security to offer the child.

Personally, I would rather see a parent live modestly on his own resources than live well with the help of others. Financial independence gives the home an integrity of its own. The child sees his family as a strong unit, secure and free, not leaning against other people or institutions. Financial independence also gives the parent more authority, since relatives and friends who offer support also tend to offer advice on childrearing. And it will tend to be difficult for you to exert your authority when doing so risks offending a benefactor.

The role of a child in a single-adult family is different from the usual role. The child should be given additional responsibilities. He should be allowed to participate in family decisions more than the child in a two-parent family. Where do we go for vacation? How will we spend the weekend? What kind of car should we buy? Should we move into another neighborhood? Can we afford a pet? The child should participate in decisions like these. I'm not saying the child should have to carry the full weight of adult responsibilities and worries at the earliest possible time, but letting a child participate in family matters can increase his sense of family, the sense of "we" that he might otherwise miss as he compares his experiences with those of other children.

This last point brings up another problem: the child's sense of self-worth. Children compare themselves to other children, and they are apt to feel inferior if they notice important differences. The divorced parent may feel completely comfortable with his status, but the child may feel that the divorce was his fault. The unwed mother may not blush at her behavior, but her child may hear whispers. This may be cruel and unfair, but it happens. Whatever the reason a child has only one parent, he is apt to need additional support to maintain good self-esteem.

The single parent may have special problems depending upon whether his status is due to divorce, death of a spouse, or being an unwed mother. I'll deal with each of these in turn.

The Divorced Parent

The fact that one out of three American marriages ends in divorce means that the development of millions of children is in the hands of single divorcees. These families are born out of crises. They are like shoots that grow at the base of a burned tree following a forest fire. No matter what the children's divorcing parents may tell them, they will feel forsaken, and will usually experience some loss of self-esteem. They may also feel guilty because they think that they either caused the divorce or that they should have been able to prevent it.

The sudden departure of a parent, usually a father, seems to represent a symbolic notification that "the king is dead." Authority is challenged and new authority must be established. This means the newly divorced parent is in for a period of intensified disobedience. Such behavior is also intensified by the child's underlying anger at one parent for leaving and at the other for having driven him away. Only if the remaining parent, in spite of his personal crisis, is able to make a firm stand, can balance be restored.

Children will usually experience increased feelings of insecurity during the weeks immediately following a divorce. Signs of nervousness such as increased sibling rivalry, whining, grouchiness, bad dreams or bed-wetting may appear. Give the child reassurance that the family will survive.

Another perplexing problem is deciding how to tell the children about an impending divorce. The most important rule is to be sure that *you* tell them rather than allowing them to find it out from someone else or simply sense it so strongly that they know without being told. If they come to feel that they aren't told things, they may develop a chronic sense of insecurity, continually wondering what *else* is going on about which they haven't been informed. A group meeting that includes all family members is the preferred setting for this truth sesssion. The children should be told when the divorce will come about, and what they can expect in the way of contact with the departing parent. They should also be encouraged to ask questions and to express their feelings.

Discreet parents will avoid negative comments about their spouses, both in the beginning and later on. A spouse's faults will speak for themselves, and the parent who points out another's failings runs the risk of incurring backlash.

And what about the parent who does not have custody? Should he try to play an important role, settle for a bit part, or can he contribute most by simply staying out of the way? Unfortunately, this parent's involvement may have nothing to do with what he has to offer. It is more likely to be a matter of how well the divorced couple is getting along, and if the children are being used as pawns in a continuing conflict. In general, I feel that the "other" parent should

133

remain involved, even when the weekend or summer visits may be inconvenient. This assures the child of a continuing exposure to adults of both sexes. Most importantly, it can soften the blows of rejection which the divorce has dealt.

Divorce always packs a tremendous emotional wallop for adults as well. The parents may have ceased to love each other. They may be told endless times, and believe it, that they are better off without their former mates. But divorcees will eventually experience a period of mourning.

For some, this period lasts only a few days or weeks. For others, it may go on for months or years. So, for a time, the divorcee is going to find it difficult to function effectively as a parent at a time when the need for parental skills is greatest. The parent may be overwhelmed by impulses to remarry immediately. Approximately two-thirds of all female divorcees remarry within eighteen months, and many of these marriages are mistakes. They only serve as a kind of anesthesia for feelings of loneliness, insecurity, or sexual tension.

Care should be taken to prevent children from becoming too attached to an adult who is not likely to be around for a sustained period. One of the most devastating experiences a child can have is to develop attachments to a new adult who then disappears. Children have already been hurt by the divorce. If they "love and lose" many more times, they'll soon develop a protective crust against committing themselves to *anyone*. This would have a devastating impact on their subsequent ability to function as a friend, a spouse, or a parent.

Finally, a word about the relationship between the child and a step-parent. If a step-child is of preschool age thorough consideration should be given to the possibility of adoption by the step-parent. The relationships of the step-parents with school age children, however, are notorious for being difficult, and are sometimes the basis for the eventual breakup of another marriage.

The step-parent of an older child should be careful not to push too hard or too fast for an intimate relationship. Often the natural parent is also anxious for the step-parent and step-child to get along famously, but the more a relationship is pushed, the more inertia is built up. Step-children must be allowed to warm up to the step-parent at their own rate, and all involved parties must be prepared for the fact that the step relationship may never be an extremely close one. If it is, that's a bonus. If it isn't, the presence of a step-parent in the home can still do much to meet the needs of the child and the previously divorced spouse.

The Death Of A Parent

Death is the only cause for single parenthood that is decreasing. Upsetting as death is, it may be more easily adjusted to than divorce, unwed pregnancy, or the adoption of a child by a single person. The death of a parent, however, will obviously produce a crisis. There will be grief, as well as a dramatic increase in the responsibilities that the bereaved parent must assume. There will inevitably be a sense of guilt, confusion and hurt on the part of the children. Still, after the immediate crisis of the funeral, the mourning, and the straightening out of family affairs, the problems of the widow or widower are similar to those of other single parents.

134

The first responsibility to confront the widow is how and what to tell the children about the death of their parent. A straight forward and honest account of how the parent died is hard to improve upon. Parents are usually better off if they respond to questions the children ask, rather than trying to anticipate what the child would like to know.

Sending a child to live with someone else during the initial mourning and adjustment is generally *not* a good idea. This can create more frustration and concern, and may cause the child to wonder what is going on when he is sent to stay with someone else on a future occasion.

The issue of a child's participation at the funeral is an extremely important one. Many adults feel it is best if children do not attend funerals and particularly if they are prevented from seeing the corpse of a dead parent. But my feeling is that most children regardless of their age should be allowed to attend the funeral of the departed parent. The reason for this is the children's ability to fantasize that the parent is not really dead. Even when they are allowed to view the corpse, the children may still have dreams or other fantasies that the parent is alive. If they are not allowed to attend the funeral, these fantasies can become obsessions. I have learned a lot from discussions with children who have lost a parent and who were not allowed to view the corpse. Many of them never gave up hope that the dead parent was still alive and would some day return. I am also acquainted with an elderly lady who, for the last thirty years, has been obsessed with the idea that her dead son might return. He was lost in a naval battle during World War II, and his body was never recovered. For decades she has fantasized that somehow her son survived the tragedy and made his way to an island. Now, over thirty years later, whenever her doorbell sounds or the phone rings, her first impulse is to think that it is the long-awaited news that her son has been rescued. Had she been able to witness the corpse of her child, life surely would have been much easier for her.

Following the funeral, it is important for both the surviving parent and the children to resolve their feelings of grief and loss. The only way this can be done is to talk about the hurt. Many parents are tempted to tell the child not to cry and not to feel badly. Nothing could be less helpful. The dead parent must be grieved for if the child's feelings are to be resolved. The matter should be discussed openly.

The problems of the widow or widower are similar to those of a divorced parent. There is a time of mourning, a period of testing parental authority, and the need to re-establish control. Widowed parents can expect insecurity on the part of the child; nothing so graphically demonstrates human frailty and the tenuousness of life as the death of a loved one.

The most important long-term need of the child is to have someone to fill the role of the departed parent. If a woman has died, the task of mothering the children can be extremely difficult. Women seem to be much more adept than men at serving as both mother and father. Finding someone to do the cooking, laundry, earn the living, mow the yard, or whatever, is only part of the problem. Someone must also provide the appropriate sex role model that would have been provided by the dead parent; someone must provide the kind of intimacy that will enable the child to relate to both men and women.

Unwed parenthood has become more socially acceptable, and many more unwed mothers are keeping their children. In some respects, the unwed parent has fewer problems than the parent who is either divorced or widowed. There is no initial crisis brought about by the departure of one parent, nor is there the red tape of going through a divorce or a funeral. There is no demand to re-establish limits and authority, nor the sudden burst of childhood insecurity which results when a parent leaves.

At the same time, there are some similar problems. The single parent suffers, along with widows and divorcees, from all of the realities associated with the fact that two heads are better than one.

And unwed parents will have a few problems that are unique to their situation. There may be assaults upon their children's self-concepts by those who disapprove of the way they were conceived or the fact that they were not placed for adoption. The unwed mother must be prepared to offer additional support to her child, to help him combat these attacks on his self-esteem.

Many single parents will find this chapter depressing. To earn a living, manage family affairs and serve as both father and mother, seem to be impossible. And, as if that were not enough, they are supposed to perform other delicate feats such as exposing a child to appropriate role models without allowing him to develop attachments that may cause him pain. True, the challenge is great. But it can be met and the child can grow into an adult with the greatest of admiration and respect for his single parent. As proof, I cite the dedication for this book.

For additional help on getting along by yourself, see the books listed below.

For an excellent review of the single parent phenomenon, which contains a number of other helpful references, see:

The Single Parent Experience by Carol Klein (Avon Books, New York, 1973).

The Adopted Family by Rondell and Michaels (Crown Publishers, New York, 1951) is a simple guide for all adopting parents, single or otherwise.

For a more scholarly treatment of the same topic, read *Shared Fate* by David Kirk (New York, Free Press, 1964).

6

The Chronically Ill Or Handicapped Child

Parents of the chronically sick or handicapped child face special problems. Their children need sensitive, patient parents who have mastered the principles of childrearing. But most of all, these kids need parents who will accept them as people, not as the embodiment of a handicap or an illness

When we see an old March of Dimes poster we see a *crippled* child. But what we forget is that the child is not *just* a handicap. The child who has a long-term illness or a handicap tends to get a new "handicapped" identity. You'll never stop everyone from thinking of your child in terms of his handicap or illness but he'll be a lot better off if at least *you* think of him as a whole person. The parent has to realize that the handicap is only one aspect—albeit an important one—of his child. If the parent comes to see the child as a handicap attached to a person, how can the child ever think of himself in any other way?

Another problem that these children have is closely related to their self-image. In chapter eighteen of the main body of the book, I talked about the importance of having good feelings about oneself. It is especially difficult for sick or handicapped children to feel good about themselves. One reason for this, as I've stated, is that people keep treating them as though they were nothing more than a handicap or a disease.

Another reason for their low esteem is that they *are* different. And those differences make life harder for them. The child with cerebral palsy cannot do for himself things that normal children of his age can easily do. The blind child cannot run and play in the same carefree way that a sighted child can. The child with leukemia does not have the boundless energy of other children. The handicap or illness is real, and the limitations it sets must be accepted. But the child should be helped to find other talents, other ways of having fun, other reasons for liking himself.

It is easy for both the child and the parent to turn away from the struggle, to surrender to the handicap or illness. It is often much easier for the parent to do things for the child than to help him do things for himself. It is also easier for the child. The parent and child often quietly agree—typically without discussing it— that the child is helpless and the parent must do everything for him.

Studies of children with congenital heart defects, for example, show that these children develop more slowly intellectually and emotionally than normal children. But there is no medical reason for their retarded development. Apparently these parents baby their children, require less of them than they would if the child were physically healthy. But such "help" is not to the child's advantage.

Parents of children with health problems must also be very careful to avoid reinforcing maladaptive behavior. A handicapped child may feel sorry for himself, refuse to try, have tantrums. The child can become an obnoxious little tyrant, and this will do nothing to improve his self-image or his enjoyment of life.

It may be a good idea to review chapter thirteen of the main body of the book, "Into the Briar Patch," since parents of handicapped or ill children are very likely to inadvertently reward undesirable behavior. They are apt, for example, to pay increased attention when he bears his burden poorly. As you know, this pattern reinforces complaining and puts "bearing up" on extinction.

The following actual case shows how the handicapped or chronically ill child can learn to become a hard-fighting adult with the courage of a seasoned mountain climber:

Peggy was one of the most interesting handicapped patients with whom I have had the pleasure of working. I did not see her until she was a thirty-year-old graduate student. Peggy's father was an alcoholic, and her mother supported the family by working as a secretary. Of necessity, Peggy had to fend for herself most of the time. This was difficult, since she was totally paralyzed from the neck down, and had been since birth.

Peggy's speech and intelligence had developed normally. By seven she had started the first grade at home. She received four and one-half hours of lessons a week on the grammar school level, but only an average of three hours per week when she reached high school. By twenty, Peggy had completed the equivalent of a high school education and received a diploma.

Between twenty and twenty-five, Peggy found herself lonesome and frustrated. She spent most of her days at home alone. Then a community person came into her life who dreamed dreams along with Peggy, dreams which saw the possibility of Peggy spreading her wings and becoming a person who could function outside of a sheltered home situation. During this period Peggy found a special gadget which enabled her to independently talk over the telephone, another breakthrough to the outside world. Equally important to her growth was when she obtained an old, beat-up electric typewriter, upon which she taught herself to type with a stick in her mouth.

Taking one small step at a time, Peggy and her friend's husband took a night course. When Peggy led the class, she next decided to try two courses. Then, the big step was taken. She and her friend went to the administration of a local college and persuaded them to admit her as a special student on a trial basis.

The family had been stripped financially over the years paying for Peggy's medical treatment, so arrangements were made by the friend to secure for Peggy a scholarship from a health agency to cover the cost of one year's tuition.

138

Eventually the state rehabilitation department was convinced to support Peggy in her undergraduate work.

When Peggy's mother learned of the plan to attend college, she was quite concerned how Peggy would be accepted on campus. She was also concerned about how Peggy would physically manage all day without her around.

Peggy only knew one person when she began Freshman Orientation, a teen-ager who had agreed to feed Peggy her lunch and push her wheelchair to various classes. This relationship did not work out, but it allowed Peggy time to make more permanent arrangements with fellow students for a small weekly fee furnished by a community group. She also made friends who wrote tests she dictated and brought her books when they went to the library for themselves. Peggy completed a four-year college course in five years, and decided to work on a master's degree in business administration. It was during her first year of graduate study that she decided to enter psychotherapy.

The six months we spent together as patient and therapist were among my most enjoyable and rewarding. There were *some* bad moments, like the time I left the room and inadvertently locked myself out. She could not, of course, let me in. In fact, she didn't even know what had happened until my face appeared at the window. Fortunately, the window was unlocked; I crawled in and our session continued.

Peggy was adept at handling stressful situations, and was not overly threatened by her impending launch into the work-a-day world. What we dealt with most in therapy was her anger and frustration at the tendency of others to see her handicap and not her personality. Most individuals actively avoided her or would look the other way when she came into view. Others tried to overcome their discomfort by being over-attentive, forever fussing about and trying to be help-ful. People who could see past her handicap, who could see *Peggy*, not Paralyzed Peggy were rare. And no matter how hard she tried, Peggy could not prevent the reactions of others from affecting her feelings as well as her self-concept.

Peggy learned to recognize and express her feelings of anger about her effect on others and her lack of truly intimate relationships. Following graduation she took an administrative position in a nearby state. She is now the sole support of her mother who is now divorced and has moved in with her.

Peggy is a rare individual, and not many people with her handicap would accomplish as much as she has. But she demonstrates very well that what holds back handicapped or chronically ill people is not so much what is wrong with themselves as it is what is wrong with those around them.

Peggy's story also illustrates the vital role creative community people often must play in order for severely handicapped children to make such progress. There is only so much most parents can do alone when they live twenty-four hours a day, day-in, day-out, with a handicapped or chronically ill child. They reach a point when community help becomes necessary.

7

The Dying Child

It happens. No one likes to think about it, but it happens. You take a perfectly healthy child in for a routine physical. Or maybe he's been a bit sluggish lately, so you take him in to see if he has a slight case of the flu. Some pills will fix him up. A shot, and he'll be as good as new. Nothing wrong with him, really.

But the physician wants to run tests. And then more tests. Then he admits the child to the hospital for closer observation and still more tests. And then it happens. They tell you that your child has leukemia. Or bone cancer. Or multiple sclerosis. Or any number of diseases you've never heard of, let alone thought might affect your child. But it happens. No one likes to think about it, but children sometimes die.

The odd thing about dying children is that their misfortune upsets the adults around them even more than it seems to bother them. Young children especially seem to be able to face death. What they have trouble with is the rejection and hostility of their parents.

It may seem strange to talk about the parents of a dying child being hostile and rejecting, but they often are. Or at least that's the way it can seem to the child. Parents and other adults often avoid a child who is terminally ill. Their impending death frightens and angers us, possibly because their illness reminds us of our own mortality, and partly because by dying they will take away something very dear to us—themselves.

Adults usually agree to a conspiracy to avoid all discussion of death or illness in the presence of the sick child. Sometimes they try to convince the child that he's perfectly all right, that nothing serious is wrong with him.

Unfortunately, these efforts do little good. I have never seen a dying child old enough to talk who didn't sense what was happening. The conspiracy does not protect the child's feelings. In fact, it adds to the child's distress, since the child senses the discomfort he causes others, their reluctance to be near him, their uneasiness.

Instead of being encouraged to express their feelings about what is happening to them, children must suppress them or risk further rejection. Since the child is denied the opportunity to deal with dying in a realistic way, he is left to his own imagination. And the child's fantasies about what is happening to him are always worse than the reality.

So the dying child is forced to live alone with his nightmares, trying desperately to find out where the truth lies, but unable to ask anyone for help. You may think that the truth is too cruel, that the kind thing to do is to delude the child into thinking that he will soon be well. I only wish that I could show you the relief that I have seen on children's faces when death was finally unmasked. Over the years I have become convinced that if a child asks about his condition he should be told. Not only that, but we should do our best to help him ask.

Sometimes a terminally ill child will live for five or more years after the disease is first diagnosed. It may be tempting in such cases to postpone the truth session until death is imminent. But I implore you to consider what may be going through the child's mind, minute by minute, day by day, as he struggles to ferret out the truth.

Once a child knows he is going to die, other questions will follow.'' What am I dying of? What will happen to me? What can I expect from life between now and the time I die? How long will I live?'' These questions should be answered honestly, but parents should also remember to reflect the feelings the questions reveal.

Dying children may have many of the same problems that the sick or handicapped child has. Even though they are blameless, parents often feel guilty about the child's illness. They bend over backwards to please the child, to make life as pleasant as they can for him. The result may be a highly dependent, spoiled, immature child.

The child who is upset by the fact that something is terribly wrong with him, combined with the fact that he cannot deal with it directly, may begin to send messages to his parents which he acts out rather than talks out. Such a child may become belligerent, uncooperative, irresponsible or overly dependent. He may regress to an earlier stage of development or pretend that he is too sick to dress and care for himself. Guilt-stricken parents often give in to these inappropriate demands. Although that may help to salve their guilt, such behavior is not in the child's best interest. It can increase his negative feelings about himself, and prevent him from developing intellectually and emotionally. Failure to grow in these areas makes death more pervasive than if it were merely a physical matter.

Spoiling a child may help to salve the parents' wounds, but their actions are not in the best interest of the child. They will not improve the child's negative feelings about himself, nor will they help him to grow intellectually or emotionally.

It is difficult for a parent to continue to be close to a dying child, to reflect feelings, to be genuine, and especially, to make demands of the child. The child needs these things more than ever but it's extremely painful to the parent to give them. The child should be helped to go as far as he can in the time that he has.

Perhaps I should say a few words about what the parents of the dying child can expect from themselves during their trial. Dr. Elizabeth Kübler-Ross, who is famous for her work with the dying, identified the stages that the parents of a dying child go through. At first the parents feel completely overwhelmed and incapable of dealing with the crisis. They tell themselves that there must be a mistake. It just can't be happening, not to them. It's simply not possible.

Then they realize that the impossible is happening, that what can't be, is. And they respond to the cruel reality with rage. Since there is no person who fills the role of enemy, the parent expresses his hostility toward his spouse, the other children, the doctors, or the dying child.

The anger is eventually replaced by guilt and frustration. The parent may be angry at himself for his inability to combat the enemy that is destroying his child. He may feel that he is worthless for having allowed this terrible thing to happen. After awhile, the anger dissipates and depression takes its place. Finally, parents reach the stage of acceptance, though they may not reach this final stage until sometime after the child has died.

No parental crisis is more trying than having a child who has been struck with a terminal disease. And there are no easy answers, no quick solutions for these parents.

I have found that parents who have lost children are more mature, stronger, more able to deal with problems honestly and directly than other parents. But to say that you will grow from this crisis, that you will be a better person for it, is no comfort to the parent who has death as an unwelcome guest in his house. But perhaps the case of James, who died of leukemia, will help pull together what I've been saying.

James was seven years old when it was first discovered that he had leukemia. After the initial diagnosis was made by a physician who specialized in hematology, the parents were asked if they would like an interview with either a chaplain or a child psychologist. They chose to see the psychologist. During the session they both expressed great concern and grief over their son's plight. They said that James had not been told about his illness and that he never would be as long as they had anything to say about it.

James was hospitalized for several days and subjected to some painful medical procedures. Eventually he was placed on a drug regimen, and one of the drugs caused him to lose his hair.

Initially he got better and was able to go home and return to school. But soon he lost considerable weight and had to return to the hospital.

James experienced two or three cycles of apparent health and relapse before his parents requested a second interview with the psychologist. They complained that, in spite of the fact that they had prayed and prayed, God had not healed their son. They felt that either they were not praying correctly, or they had not been good enough for God to answer their prayers. Yet they still refused to give up hope that James would be healed.

Of more immediate concern was the fact that James now refused to dress himself or to leave the house. He would not go to Sunday School, on shopping trips with his mother or even for rides with his father. He insisted on staying in bed and often cried if his mother left his room for even a few minutes. At night, when he was supposed to go to bed, he refused to sleep. He demanded to stay up and watch TV after his parents had retired. They had permitted this, and each night he would fall asleep on the couch. The family would awaken the next morning to find James in the living room asleep with the television still on.

During the second visit, the parents agreed to come for weekly sessions. After a few of these interviews, they were able to openly admit some of their despair and anger. They also expressed concerns about demands which James and his illness had placed on them. Admitting to these feelings seemed to free the parents to examine ways of dealing with the childrearing problems that had emerged.

James' parents soon began to demand that he dress himself and go to school when he felt well. And, he was no longer allowed to stay up late or to sleep on the couch. His mother stopped spending every moment with him and began doing a better job of meeting her other responsibilities as a homemaker and wife.

To the parents' surprise, all of this seemed to make them feel relieved, and without the sense of overwhelming guilt they felt they would have. Soon they were giving more honest and genuine support to their critically ill son, and the time they *did* spend with him was more pleasant. James also became less anxious and seemed happier.

One of the most important meetings between the parents and psychologist occurred when James had been re-admitted to the hospital. The parents asked the psychologist if he would be willing to discuss death with their son. They felt it was time for James to know he was going to die, but they could not bring themselves to tell him.

In his meeting with James, the psychologist said empathically, "You seem to be worried about what is going to happen to you." To this James responded, "I am going to die, aren't I?" "Yes," responded the psychologist, "I was sure you knew."

The remainder of the discussion dealt primarily with James' feelings of fear and anger, but after a short cry, James said he felt relieved just to know for sure what was wrong with him.

James died after an illness of eighteen months. In the weeks before his death, he seemed only very tired, but not unhappy or frightened.

Following the funeral, the parents scheduled a final interview with the psychologist. They said that they knew they had done everything they could for James, and this seemed to relieve them of any lingering guilt. They also expressed the confidence that, although his illness and death had brought terrible grief, they were adjusting to the reality of having to give him up.

144

8

Pandora's Box

As a consultant to parents and as a parent myself, I encounter certain problems repeatedly. These, I feel, deserve a measure of special attention. I've included them in this last chapter as a smorgasbord of challenges to your skills that you can most certainly count on sampling during your parental career. The subjects range from the universal parental necessity of helping a young child deal with fears, through guiding adolescents as they accept responsibility for a car, to problems of runaways and the difficult, painful choices their parents must make. Every parent will sample at least one or two of these challenges; they're part of the job description.

Thumbsucking

Theories about thumbsucking are as varied as the fingerprints of those nursed-upon digits. Some say it results from not having sufficient sucking experiences in infancy; others feel that children who are allowed to suck too much develop the habit. The most credible theory of thumbsucking, however, is that the parents' reaction to this behavior is what maintains it. If this is true, the reinforcement may be increased attention: it upsets us and thus allows children to manipulate and control not only what we pay attention to, but how we feel. This theory is supported by the fact that one of the most successful ways of treating thumbsucking is to administer tranquilizers to the *parents*! The resulting "I could care less" attitude undoubtedly removes whatever mysterious reinforcement the parents are providing.

Thus, in most cases of thumbsucking the best maneuver is to ignore it completely. If thumbsucking has been responded to properly at an early age, the child will not suck his thumb after growing his permanent teeth. But if he does, it can cause dental problems. Parents who find themselves unable to manage the problem of thumbsucking after permanent teeth begin to appear should seek the help of an effective dental or mental health practitioner.

Some fears come about naturally. If a child is bitten by a dog, he may develop an aversion to all furry animals. Other fears are communicated to the child; the mother who gets upset every time it thunders may produce a child who runs and hides when it storms. Some fears persist because they are rewarded. A frightened child may get more attention, or he may be allowed to sleep between Mommy and Daddy. Parents who themselves were often frightened as children are the most likely to over-react and thereby reinforce the child's fearfulness.

Parents who avoid becoming overly embroiled in their children's fears seem to be the most capable of helping. A fearful child needs acceptance and empathic understanding. Parents, however, should make it clear that they do not share the fear. They should be able to understand and accept how the child feels without buying the idea that this fear is reality based. Parents who simply ignore the child's fear rob him of badly needed support, but parents who over-attend, or who act as though the fear could be real, are liable to reinforce it.

If properly handled, most fears will subside. They may re-occur during times of stress; for instance, children commonly develop a fear of the dark when they first begin school. By the same token, adolescents may manifest symbolic fears caused by the increase in sexual impulses. A certain number of fears are normal; if parents do not reinforce them, they should disappear in time. If fears seem abnormally intense, or if they persist for months, professional help should be sought.

Enuresis and Encopresis

To say bedwetting (enuresis) is a common problem is to excel at the fine art of understatement. The most reliable statistics indicate that as many as one out of every four children between the ages of four and sixteen years have this problem at one time or another. The overwhelming majority of bedwetters (in excess of ninety percent) do not suffer from any kind of organic bladder or urinary tract problem. Research suggests that many of them experience stages of exceedingly deep sleep. This somehow allows their sphincter muscles to relax, causing wetting without even waking up. There is little evidence to suggest that all or even a majority of bedwetters have emotional problems that cause this difficulty. That does not, however, give any assurance that emotional problems might not be caused by the bedwetting.

Methods of treating enuresis are as numerous as the gray hairs it has caused. Some parents mistakenly make a direct attack by criticizing or punishing the enuretic child. Others try to reason with him or to get him to "try harder." For effectiveness, these methods are tied for last place with the threat to castrate him, which amazingly, is still voiced in some homes. Many enuretics have been given counseling and psychotherapy, but this form of treatment is usually not of great benefit. Some success has been achieved by limiting the amount of fluid a child can drink prior to bedtime and by requiring him to urinate before he goes to sleep. There are medications which have been somewhat successful in treating bedwetting and which can be prescribed by the child's pediatrician.

The most successful means of dealing with bedwetting has been the "pad and bell" technique. This method involves a device which turns on a light and rings a bell in order to awaken a child when he urinates. The bell and light help sensitize him to the fullness of his bladder or to a sphincter muscle that is about to relax. Such an awareness can startle him awake when he is about to urinate. During the first few days on such a program the child will usually continue to wet, but the resulting spot will grow increasingly smaller. After a week or two he will be dry for one night, then for two or three nights in a row. After ten to twelve weeks the child should remain continuously dry.

There are companies that sell the pad and bell program to parents. Some of them are reputable while others are not. Some set appropriate fees and others try to break the bank. The best service is usually obtained from a Ph.D. or M.D. who uses this approach rather than from a salesman, but many doctors are not knowledgeable in this technique and therefore cannot provide it. Parents wishing further information on the pad and bell technique should have their family physician or psychologist contact the Pediatric Psychology Clinic of Oklahoma Children's Memorial Hospital, Oklahoma City, Oklahoma 73190.

"Encopretic" is the medical term for a child who defecates in his clothing, and the incidence of this problem is much higher than most laymen would suspect. One physician has written a report on one hundred thirty-eight children whom he has treated. I personally receive about one referral per week for this problem. About nineteen out of every twenty children who soil, do so for psychological reasons. Hirschsprung's disease, the absence of nerve cells in the lower bowel, is about the only major organic cause of encopresis.

Surprisingly, soiling is seldom caused by children who deliberately expel feces; more often it results from retention of stools. Prolonged retention produces an impacted and distended bowel. If distention persists, megacolon (permanent distention) will result. Bowel movements then become infrequent, with stools extremely large and painful to pass. Unfortunately, most children with encopresis retain stools for a long time before their parents seek help. At that point the soiling is very difficult to reverse, and few practitioners possess the skill necessary to treat such a complex behavioral-medical problem. If parents would only seek professional help when their child first begins to pass large and infrequent stools, most cases of encopresis could be prevented.

By far the best method for treating fecal soiling is the judicious use of rewards and punishments in combination with suppository laxatives. Encopretic children are required to defecate each day, usually in the morning. They may do this voluntarily, with the assistance of glycerine suppositories, or with the aid of an enema if necessary. They receive a reward for every time they defecate in the toilet, and for going a specified period of time, such as a day, without soiling. An appropriate punishment can be administered for each incidence of soiling. The suppositories and enemas keep the child's colon evacuated, and allow it to regain its normal shape and tone. The rewards and punishments encourage appropriate toilet behavior. These two factors in combination are usually the treatment of choice, but no parent should undertake such a program without the assistance of a skilled behavioral or medical practitioner. Parents wanting aid in treating an encopretic child could also have their physician or psychologist write us.

The response by parents can have a lot to do with whether or not the wetting or soiling gets better or worse. We should be careful not to inadvertently reward (by increasing attention or by becoming upset) the child's wetting or soiling. We should be especially alert to opportunities for providing rewards for not wetting and not soiling. As parents, we may make the child feel as though he is some kind of a cross between Judas and Benedict Arnold, and nothing is gained by causing him to dislike himself.

Sibling Rivalry

As sure as there are siblings, there is going to be sibling rivalry. The issue is not whether or not, but its degree. Generally speaking, the less the sibling rivalry, the better. Still, in some homes, strong negative feelings exist between siblings but remain unexpressed. Here the absence of overt rivalry is no cause for rejoicing, since the emotional problems still exist for which rivalry is a symptom. Parents should not be concerned by moderate amounts of rivalry such as occasional bickering and fighting. But if rivalry is the theme of family life, this may be symptomatic of emotional troubles, in addition to the fact that it places an embargo on happiness and enjoyment in the home.

One common occurrence not commonly recognized as sibling rivalry involves regression of an older child, say a four-year-old, when a sibling is born. He may return to sucking his thumb, wanting to sleep in the baby's bed, wetting or soiling himself and talking baby talk. This phenomen will usually go away in a few days if parents do not overreact.

In considering what to do about sibling rivalry, parents should begin by asking if there is any way in which "getting into it" is paying off for the kids. Quite often the answer is "Yes." It may be a means by which they get increased attention, or it can be a great way for siblings to manipulate and control their parents. If a parent becomes upset, then the little rivaler is controlling what the parent feels, what he is thinking about and what he is doing. Sibling encounters can also be a way of draining off angry and hostile emotions. When this happens, parents will need to teach the children more acceptable ways of expressing their negative feelings.

Proper structure or limit-setting can help produce a cease fire between sibs. Each child should be informed that he will not be allowed to exploit a sibling, and the consequences for same should be clearly set forth. Then if a child breaks one of these rules, he should be punished in a matter-of-fact way, but *without the parents becoming upset*. Also, parents must be careful never to let an offender get off without a response. If this happens he will probably strike again and the victim will lose his confidence in law and order. He may then resort to vigilante tactics and, "Here we go again!"

148

Eating problems can take two widely diverse forms. One usually involves a child who won't eat and the other involves the child with a weight problem. Refusal to eat, like thumbsucking, head banging and numerous other forms of maladaptive behavior, will usually not occur unless there is outside interference. The fact is, there's nothing great about going hungry. Children don't eat because they have found that this can be a way of controlling adults. And the child who's hooked on manipulation of parents is, like any other addict, always willing to give up his lunch in order to feed his habit.

Many middle-class parents are easy prey for their fasting rather than feasting children. This is because feeding is one of the few ways they know to fulfill their role as parents. If they knew more about applying the principles of behavior they probably wouldn't be so concerned about their child's caloric intake. Parents who have only a skillet in their bag of tricks will communicate to the child that eating is something of great importance to *them*. This, of course, obscures the child's awareness of how important eating is for him, and this can be devastating as far as the principle of responsibility (chapter twenty) is concerned.

The best eating policy for most homes is simply to serve nourishing meals and assume that, if left alone, children will eat rather than starve themselves to death. But, should the child not eat properly or at all, some minor adjustments may be in order. Parents should then serve the child's plate with a well-balanced meal and tell him if he cleans it he can have seconds, dessert, and can eat between meals. If he does not clean his plate, or even eat a crumb, that's okay. But the "no eating" consequences are enforced without exception. This procedure invariably works, and I have yet to lose a child to starvation in such a program. The difficulty is getting parents to carry out the program carefully. They must refrain from coaxing, and they have to make sure that the child does not sneak between-meal snacks. For some parents, the price for staying on their toes like this is too high. It's like asking for half their kingdom and their daughter's hand in marriage. They don't want to work that hard or take the responsibility necessary to make sure it works. They'd rather just give in and hope the opposition will settle for half the kingdom.

Getting children to eat is sometimes not the problem. An increasing number of them are overweight. This can have a grave effect on their health and motivation to work; besides, children who are allowed to become little fatties during the preadolescent years may develop irreversibly bad self images.

No problem of human functioning which is so simple, has been distorted into a more complex difficulty, than has overweight. Any endocrinologist will tell you that in the overwhelming majority of cases, weight is a direct result of the number of calories an individual takes in and the number he burns up. By the most generous estimates, the number of people who are overweight because of any kind of glandular difficulty range from almost no one up to a maximum of ten percent.

There are thousands of old wives tales about the causes of overweight and the cures for them. These are fostered by everything from poorly conceived maga-

149

zine articles to quacks. But the truth of the matter is that the only things a person can do to lose weight are: (1) control caloric intake by controlling the amount he eats; (2) burn up calories with carefully conceived programs of exercise and exertion; (3) consume calories which are generally not stored (protein) as opposed to calories which are stored (carbohydrates and fats).

In spite of all the fancy diets one hears about, the most successful weight loss programs are about as exotic as your last passport photo. They are modeled after the programs employed by interscholastic wrestlers who must rid themselves of every last ounce of fat. Throughout the U.S., there are thousands of high school and college boys who, though by no means fat, are routinely able to trim off one pound or more per day. Many of them who play football at a trim 200 pounds plus can drop below 150 pounds in less than six weeks in order to compete in wrestling. And, this is done without injuring their health or even making them weak. Thus, any man, woman or child is capable of doing the same thing if he *wants* to lose weight as badly as a wrestler wants to be on the team.

The most successful weight loss program for children referred to our hospital involves a variation of the wrestler's program plus rewards and punishments. It was applied to Tina, a fifteen-year-old highschool junior who lived with her father and stepmother. The parents sought professional help after they realized her 5'2" frame was carrying a load of 170 pounds. They had previously focused their attention on her intellectual and personality development, they had given her coaching on how to relate to other individuals, and had always encouraged her to make good grades. Now the parents had reached a point where they felt something should be done about her physical development, but they really didn't know what to do.

The parents were warned that getting another person to lose weight is a difficult task. I explained that an adolescent of Tina's age would probably rebel against the program. Nonetheless, they insisted that they would feel irresponsible if they did not follow through with the best weight loss program available during the two remaining years before Tina went away to college. She could then decide for herself whether she wanted to maintain a low weight or return to the level of obesity of her choice.

A program was set up which consisted of approximately ten different exercises, plus jogging. It began with nonstrenuous activity, which increased in difficulty as her muscles rounded into shape. The whole thing required only fifteen to thirty minutes per day. A high protein diet was prescribed. It consisted of a hard-boiled egg or dry cereal for breakfast, a small bowl of soup for lunch, and broiled fish or chicken (without skin) plus one cooked and one raw vegetable for supper. The diet allowed one pint of milk per day and all of the diet drinks and coffee or tea (without sugar and cream) that the patient desired. There was no eating between meals.

Tina was given fifty cents for each day she did her exercises. A new phone was installed in her room and a listing taken out in her name. Each week that she lost two and one half pounds or more, she was allowed unrestricted use of the phone. She was also permitted unlimited use of the family car. If Tina did not do her exercises or if she did not lose her two and a half pounds per week, her telephone and car privileges were suspended, and she was forced to spend thirty minutes every afternoon helping her mother with chores. The mother soon discovered a particularly effective punishment, making Tina do chores her younger half-brother and half-sister were normally required to perform.

At first, Tina lost three to five pounds almost every week without much difficulty. After about a month, however, she began to resist the eating and exercise program, and eventually stopped losing weight. She maintained her weight for a couple of weeks and then began to gain a few pounds. Finally, Tina announced that she could not bear having the weight program and its consequences imposed upon her. Unless it was removed, she threatened to go to live with her natural mother. The parents responded by saying they they wanted very much for her to stay, but that the program would not be discontinued. Tina proceeded to move out, but only for one week. After that she returned home and re-entered the weight loss program. From that time forward she lost approximately two and a half pounds per week until she achieved a weight of 120 pounds. She is now a college student living outside the home, weighing under 125 pounds. Parents wishing more information on this exercise or diet regime should have their physician or psychologist write me.

Household Chores

Today's home, unlike the agricultural family of the past generations, is not dependent on children's labor. Quite to the contrary, many modern children suffer from not having any really useful work to perform. For this reason, most parents require help around the house primarily for the purpose of teaching children a sense of responsibility. But it would be easier for many parents to pass through the eye of a needle than to go through the ordeals of getting a child to do chores.

Each child needs responsibilities, however, if his character is to develop optimally. Work that fosters responsibility can include maintaining one's own room, helping with general house cleaning or working in the yard. A family garden can be a great asset in teaching responsibility as well as a source of future enjoyment. Responsibility for feeding and otherwise caring for pets is encouraged.

If chores are assigned, children will learn one of two things. Either they will develop the necessary self-discipline and discover the benefits of responsibility, or they will learn how to manipulate parents and how to avoid work like the cracks in a sidewalk. Parents should follow the same principles with chores as they do with other rules: that is, the nature of the responsibility should be crystal clear. This includes not only whose job it is to dump the trash, but by what hour it is to be carried out. Some parents' rules are about as easily understood as the instructions for your tax form.

The rewards that children receive will obviously influence how well they carry out their chores. And many parents work against themselves by inadvertently rewarding footdragging or downright disobedience. For instance, if nonperfor-

151

mance of duty "drives us up the wall" this response of the drivee will likely be rewarding to the driver. By not carrying out the garbage, the child may manipulate us into: (1) becoming upset, (2) giving him increased attention, and (3) assuming responsibility by reminding him several times what he should be doing. Under these conditions,the child learns only how to be dragged kicking and screaming into the performance of any duty.

Parents who fail to give their child an allowance are passing up a great source of rewards and punishments for chore-related, as well as other, behaviors. Parents who provide an allowance without making it contingent on the performance of specific duties, make the same mistake. Remember, a good reward (or punishment) is one that works. If a twenty-five cent fine isn't enough, up the stakes.

As parents in the last half of the twentieth century, it is increasingly difficult to teach responsibility. A young person today who truly understands responsibility is about as rare as the *cold center of my old aunt Myrtle's roast beef* (Uncle Bill used to complain that he'd "seen cows burned worse than that, and get well."). The consequences of rearing a generation of irresponsible children have become greater and greater. Carefully conceived programs of chores can be an important part of the solution of this problem.

The Telephone

It is amazing that an instrument as small as the telephone can cause such large problems. Like the atom bomb and the exhaust-spewing automobile, the telephone stands as a classic example of a technological advance which has produced more than its share of social and ecological disturbances. In most homes, the basis for telephone difficulties is lack of structure. The child is often not told clearly when and how much he should be allowed to use this instrument he regards as so vital to his sense of fulfillment. But in spite of their failure to provide clear limits, parents often complain that the phone is used too much or at the wrong time.

If lack of structure is the main reason for telephone-related problems, then the solution must lie in providing it. Parents should set rules about when and how much the phone can be used, and then stick to them. If children cannot use the phone until after their homework or chores are done, then these rules should be enforced. If parents need the line kept open for family calls, then they should tell the children they cannot talk or that they must limit their calls. Most children don't mind following rules that are clearly spelled out. What they do object to is being told to get off the phone right in the middle of a conversation which, to them, is second in importance only to the message Paul Revere got from the tower of the Old North Church. By the way, almost all adolescent conversations with peers fall within that category.

Cars, Motorcycles, and Other Potential Dangers

One aspect of the issue of responsibility is how much children will be allowed to expose themselves to danger. Problems of this type usually crop up around issues like: (1) Will the child be allowed to have a motorcycle? (2) Will he be permitted to have or even drive a car? (3) What about guns, lawnmowers, and other potentially dangerous equipment? The answer to these questions, like all great wisdom, is not held by a guru from the East. It is found within our principles of behavior: (1) children must be allowed, even required, to assume responsibility (chapter twenty); (2) parents should not be phonies, and thus they should never subsidize any behavior in which they do not believe (chapter nineteen); (3) parents must present a unified approach (chapter fourteen).

Although some parents will disagree, it is my firm belief that a teenager should be allowed to do anything that he can pay for, that does not infringe upon the rights of others, and that does not break the law. This means that a child who earns the money to buy a gun or a motorcycle should be allowed to have one, as long as he is old enough to obtain the necessary licenses. He is entitled to instruction on the proper use of the potentially dangerous equipment. At the same time, he is also entitled to freedom from lecturing and moralizing on such matters. The best way to determine what is necessary and what is unnecessary teaching, is to check how much repetition is involved. Continued warnings can distract children from worrying about how much they have at stake, and into obsession about what others might think. Parents should not contribute money to a purchase (e.g., a gun or motocycle) if they have personal objections to it. But it is equally bad to nag, distract and otherwise usurp responsibility from a child who does acquire such items. Some parents manage to make both mistakes. That is, they allow themselves to be talked into buying something that they really don't believe the child should have. Then they nag like a fishwife about how he uses it.

Children who are allowed to operate dangerous equipment may get hurt. That's a reality we cannot change. But children who are forbidden to have guns or vehicles may develop an affinity for them. They can become like the son of a couple with whom I consulted recently, whose problem was labeled "Hondaphilia." Such children usually get what they want in spite of their parents, but without a sense of responsibility having been built in along the way. They would be better off if they had been taught the proper use of such equipment. Children who learn that it is their responsibility to keep from injuring themselves are likely to be truly cautious and responsible. Parents who continually nag, snoop and otherwise interfere, teach their children to sneak around. This can produce the most irresponsible and dangerous behaviors.

Runaways

It's been said that being the parents of an adolescent is like riding a roller coaster: you'd like to get off and be sick, but everyone keeps telling you how much fun it is. Probably no parent has less fun, and is more profoundly aware of the pain involved, than the one whose child threatens to run away.

Running away is an increasing problem because of the nature of parent/child relationships today. Kids have more money, and there are young people's communities that will take in runaways. In spite of these changes, running away is a violation of the law in almost every state. The most typical runaway is a child from a middle class home who leaves for only a few days or weeks.

Running away is seldom a means of escaping an oppressive situation; it is more likely a means of manipulating parents. Most middle class parents are as intimidated as Chicken Little when their child threatens to leave. They interpret this as a symbol of their failure, and are often more concerned about what others will think of them than they are about the welfare of their child. They usually do not understand why the child wants to go, and greatly overestimate the desirability of living outside the home from the child's point of view.

One of my most difficult functions as a childrearing consultant is to help parents gain a degree of objectivity in perceiving and responding to runaway situations. It is usually a desperate act on the part of a young person to communicate something to his parents which he has tried and tried to tell them, but which they have not heard. This "something" can range from "Stop meddling in my business, and let me live my own life," to "Won't someone please tell me exactly what the rules are?" Most runaways are in the thirteen to sixteen age bracket. This period, of course, corresponds to a critical stage of development known as adolescence. A child at this age has a burning need to develop his *own* sense of identity, and to acquire a feeling of independence. Sometimes a wanderlust promises an answer to all these questions.

All of these explanations notwithstanding, what are parents supposed to do if their child runs away or threatens to do so? To begin with, they should structure a step-by-step program for remedying the situation. The orderliness and deliberateness of parental action is emphasized because of the temptation of many of them to burst into extensive but diffuse action. Step one should involve a sober self-examination and an assessment of the home situation. "Sober" means objective, not a guilt-ridden underestimation of one's self and the home. You should also be careful not to become defensive in a way that causes you to overestimate your parental virtues. Parents may need the help of a counselor in order to make such an appraisal.

Parents will need to evaluate how well the most sound rules of behavior are being followed. How well are the parents facilitating communication? Have they set themselves up as easy prey for manipulation and thereby encouraged the child to run away? Are they giving consent or even subsidizing things in which they do not personally believe? The parents of most children who threaten to run away usually give the wrong answers to these questions. They may need help in setting limits and in using rewards and punishments correctly. Or they may not be listening effectively.

With or without professional help, the home should be put in order. This inevitably means more stringent demands will be made of the child in some areas, and greater freedom will be given in others. For instance, the parents may need to stop giving the child money or increase his chores on the one hand, while getting off his back about his values or how he spends his *own* time, on the other. When the necessary corrections in the home atmosphere are made, then comes the greatest risk and challenge of all: giving the child an honest choice of whether to live at home or to leave if he finds it intolerable. Parents must be careful to avoid presenting this alternative in either a rejecting, "Just leave, see if I care" or seductive, "You know your mother and I are praying for you to stay" manner. It should also be understood that, if the child leaves, the parents will *not* contribute money, clothing, or any other material support.

Any parent confronted with the reality or the prospect of a runaway will have to do a great deal of soul searching to decide whether or not he wants to give his child true freedom of choice to live at home or stay away. In the overwhelming majority of cases, children who are given such choices elect to stay at home. Some parents, however, in order to satisfy their own needs or because of their lack of confidence in their children, feel that they must manipulate the child into staying at home. They are the most likely to create an atmosphere which thwarts the child's development, and which incites him to run away. Genuinely loving a child, while at the same time allowing him to make his own choices (bad ones as well as good ones), is the highest and purest form of love. Maximizing a child's development requires the parents to take risks. A refusal to risk may be a short cut to developmental delay and family dissension. Even in cases where a child decides to leave, the benefits gained by this freedom and responsibility may be the best thing for him.

The case of Kim provides a typical illustration of a runaway situation. She was a pretty high school junior who had always been popular and successful. She had made straight A's in every class since the fifth grade, was an outstanding tennis player and cheerleader, and had been elected to every school honor she had ever sought. At the time Kim ran away, she was dating the most popular boy in her class. He was an outstanding athlete, but extremely domineering in his relationship with her.

Kim's father was a businessman who got along well with everyone, including his own children. The mother had gone back to college, and was in her first year of teaching when Kim ran away. She had pushed Kim to achieve in school and sports, as well as to be popular with boys and in school politics. Kim had always measured up to the expectations of others, including church people who had told her that she should dedicate her whole life to God and the church. A factor which undoubtedly contributed more than any other to Kim's running away was this intense pressure she felt to perform for others. How she yearned to be out from under it all!

Things started going downhill fast when Kim's parents decided that she and her boyfriend were not good for each other. Kim was required to tell her parents where she was, and what she was doing, every moment she was away from home. She soon improved her capacity for lying because this seemed easier than enduring the ordeals that followed when she told the truth. She began to miss church, stay out late, and eventually started coming home intoxicated from alcohol or other drugs.

The second time Kim came home drunk, the mother kept her up all night questioning her. The next day Kim left and did not contact her parents for three days. She then called and said she had been living with a college student but wished to move in with her widowed grandmother.

In the meantime, Kim's parents had sought professional help. They readily . confessed to being total failures as parents and stated they would do anything to get Kim back. They were somewhat surprised when the psychologist encouraged them to do a better job of enforcing their rules, but to let up on Kim in other ways. The psychologist also encouraged them to provide a psychotherapist for Kim, since her behavior indicated at least a moderate degree of emotional disturbance.

Much consultation time was spent in coaching Kim's parents on how to butt out of Kim's life. The mother was able to gain some awareness of how she was trying to use her daughter to attain some of her *own* goals and how this constituted a threat to Kim's privacy and to her sense of responsibility. It was decided that the parents would forbid the grandmother to keep Kim. They would make their home as effective as possible, then leave it up to Kim whether she lived there or went out on her own. Some of the changes involved relieving Kim of having to continually tell her parents where she was and what she was doing. She was required to be in by 10:00 every evening Sunday through Thursday. On Friday and Saturday she was allowed to be out until 1:00 if she wished. Anytime she stayed out after curfew, she was denied one night out for each fifteen minutes she was late.

Kim's parents also told her that they felt reasonably sure she was using her allowance and lunch money for tobacco, alcohol and possibly other drugs of which they did not approve. They therefore stated that she would not receive any more allowance until they were satisfied that she was not using it for such purposes. Kim was allowed to fix her own lunch and to take it to school since the parents were uncomfortable that lunch money might also be diverted for drugs.

Kim's feelings about the new rules were mixed. The "no money" policy was hard to accept, but freedom to drive the family automobile and not having to tell her parents where she was all the time were appreciated. So, Kim decided to try living at home. Much to her own surprise, the mother was able to stick to her promise of not bothering Kim about where she was or who she was with. The mother also developed a new respect for Kim's autonomy and seldom lectured her on any topic. Both parents took an "It's up to you" attitude towards Kim's friends, dates, whether or not she ran for office, her studies, her tennis and her cheerleading. Strangely enough, this seemed a little hard for Kim to take, and on occasion she tried to manipulate her parents into making some of these decisions for her. A few weeks after moving back home, Kim confessed to her parents about her experimentation with drugs. But she said that she had quit, and asked if she could have her allowance restored. The parents decided to trust her and the allowance was reinstated.

At present Kim is a high school senior. She is taking only half-time courses, since she needs only a few credits to graduate. She still makes good grades, but has given up competitive tennis. She now dates several boys, and her main requirement of any future boyfriend or husband is that he not be domineering. Kim has dropped out of church, although she says she has not given up God or religion. She states that she simply needs to work out her own religious commitments rather than having other people tell her what to do. Kim plans to attend college but to live at home, and her relationship with her parents is now regarded as "above average" by all parties involved.

As I prepare to write my final words, I have a familiar feeling. It is the same sensation I have experienced in parent consultation groups when our sessions were almost over. In addition to the sadness of parting, I always felt a need to provide closure by making some appropriate parting remark. I usually thank them for letting me try to walk in their shoes. But I always confessed that there was no way to achieve closure on the issue of childrearing. It is a continuous process of personal growth and of increasing one's skill and understanding. I can only hope that through this book I may have planted a few seeds. If they are sown in fertile minds, then with the showers of unwavering reflection and practice, fruit will come forth.

Author and Subject Index

Consequences of behavior, 47, 53, 99-106, 149, 151
Consistency
  importance of in rewards, 35-38, 61-65
  in rule enforcement, 111-113
Control
  impulses, 122
  of children's behavior, 1-3, 131
  of parent by child by making angry, 43
  of rewards by parents, 39
  parental responsibility for, 2
  parent to parent communication about, 3, 4
Corporal punishment
  proper application of, 51, 52-55
  limitations of, 37, 51
Correction
  advantages of, 49, 50
  disadvantages of, 49, 52
  for dangerous behavior, 52
  principle of, 49
  to discourage behavior, 89
Creativity, 1, 2, 60

Decisions
  by child, 99-106
    about leaving home, 155, 156
    related to drugs, 121-126
  child's participation in, 2, 99-106, 132, 155, 156
  by child of single parent, 132
  moral and religious, 127-130
Death
  of a child, 141-144
  of a parent, 131, 134, 135
Delayed gratification by saving of tokens, 23
Discipline
  reasoning as, 8, 9, 38, 54
  reinforcement as, 11-20, 21-26, 27-29, 31-34, 35-39, 41-43, 45-48, 49-55, 57-60, 61-65, 138, 145-156
  spanking as, 37, 43, 51-55, 62
Divorce, how to tell the children, 133
Divorced parents, 132, 133, 134
Drugs
  alcohol, 58, 122, 123, 125, 126, 155, 156
  abuse of, 32, 112, 121-126, 155, 156
  decision making regarding, 121, 126
  education regarding, 121-126

facts about, 125, 126
heroin, 2, 58, 123, 125, 126
inhalants, 121, 123, 125
marijuana, 112, 121, 123, 125
psychedelic, 121, 123, 125
sedatives, 121, 122
stimulants, 121, 123, 126
tobacco, 31, 32, 122, 125, 126, 156

Eating problems, 149-151
Empathy
  demonstration of, 70-72, 82-86, 88, 89, 104
  in dealing with dying child, 144
  parental fear of, 84, 85
Encopresis (soiling), 146-148
Enuresis (bedwetting), 146-148
Existential neurosis, 67
Extinction
  of undesired behavior, 35-39, 52, 62-64
  temporary relapse after, 38
  used in Time Out, 43

Family
  importance of intimacy in, 67-73, 122
  strong sense of, 132, 133
Fears
  empathy in dealing with, 70, 71
  of death, 144
  proper handling, 146
Feelings
  honesty of, 93-97
  importance of child's, 87-91
    about divorce, 132, 133
    about his impending death, 141-144
  of divorced parents, 134
  of grief and loss in death, 135
  of guilt, 54, 55, 77, 78, 83, 84, 95, 96, 133, 134, 142-144, 154
  of handicapped children, 137-139
  of inadequacy, 94, 95, 122
  of parents, 93
  of safety in parent-child relationship, 67, 68, 76, 79
  reflecting, 81-86, 89, 90, 94, 95, 142
  verbalizing negative, 96, 97, 148
Finances
  of parents of handicapped children, 138
  of single parents, 132
Fines
  advantage of, 45, 46, 58

161

163